D1478460

SLAVISTIC PRINTINGS AND REPRINTINGS

edited by

C. H. VAN SCHOONEVELD

Indiana University

211

Koz'ma Prutkov. A lithography of L. M. Žemčužaikov, A. E. Beideman, and
L. F. Lagorio, 1853 – 1854.

KOZ'MA PRUTKOV
the Art of Parody

by

BARBARA HELDT MONTER

1972
MOUTON
THE HAGUE · PARIS

© Copyright 1972 in The Netherlands.
Mouton & Co. N.V. Publishers, The Hague.

LIBRARY OF CONGRESS CATALOG CARD NUMBER: 71–190144

Printed in Hungary

for Rolfe Humphries

PREFACE

The theory and literary history of parody have always overstepped national boundaries. Theory of literature must deal with all of literature, and parodists are generally well-read. Gifted parodists such as W. B. Scott, writing in the United States today, are as fully capable of ridiculing André Gide as they are of parodying the style of our home-grown writers. But parody itself usually claims only a national audience; its connection with a specific language is too intimate. Such has been the fate of Koz'ma Prutkov. He is, as I hope to show, too universal a figure to remain largely in Russia and in Russian.

In working with Prutkov I have translated many of his poems into English verse. Rhyme is an essential ingredient of Prutkovian humor. Without rhyme, doggerel cannot exist; it is literally "rhyme without reason". Perfection of execution goes hand in hand with triviality of subject matter. Much of the clarity and smoothness of his absurdity has been lost, but I hope that something of Prutkov will come through into English.

The relationships of parody to the history of Russian literature, that of parody to all of literature, and that of literature to biography and social history are discussed here only insofar as they focus on the phenomenon of Koz'ma Prutkov. These matters have been and will be taken up by other scholars. My intention is to do justice to Prutkov as one of the first steps in this long and fascinating literary journey.

B. Ja. Buxštab and Frank Ingram generously shared their own knowledge of Prutkov with me. The librarians and archivists of the institutions where I worked (the University of Chicago Library, the Lenin Library in Moscow, C.G.A.L.I., and the Puškinskij dom) helped me tremendously. A Fulbright grant and the support of the Inter-University Committee on Travel Grants enabled me to visit these places. I wish to thank Ralph Matlaw, Hugh McLean, Edward Stankiewicz and Richard Wortman for their extremely valuable comments on slightly different versions of this book. A generous grant from the Committee on Slavic Area Studies of the University of Chicago made its publication possible. Sufficient tribute cannot be paid to my husband, who always assumed it would be excellent.

Chicago, December 1970 Barbara Heldt Monter

TABLE OF CONTENTS

INTRODUCTION

The literary humor of a nation is perhaps its most perishable cultural export. The humorous writings of Aleksej Tolstoj and the Brothers Žemčužnikov, known to the Russian reading public under the pseudonym of Koz'ma Prutkov, have been as popular in Russia[1] as they have been unknown abroad.[2] To his admirers, Koz'ma Prutkov is not a mere pseudonym; he is an entire personage, and his personality is inseparable from his works. Prutkov is a bureaucrat who also writes poetry. His love for the most oppressive, stale, and inhuman aspects of Nicholas I's Russia is combined with a conviction that his writings are destined for immortality. He unites the tyrannic pride of the official with the blatant smugness of the hack poet, but because of the sublime guiltlessness that Comedy bestows upon all her great incarnations, he has been equally beloved by his contemporaries and by Russians of today. In a letter of February 27, 1883[3] to the distinguished literary historian A. N. Pypin, Vladimir Žemčužnikov wrote that Koz'ma Prutkov, "living and

---

[1] The *Complete Works* of Koz'ma Prutkov, edited by A. M. and V. M. Žemčužnikov, first published in 1884, were reprinted eleven times before 1917. There have been several enlarged editions since then: one in 1927 (edited by B. Tomaševskij and K. Xalabaeva), the "Academia" edition of 1933 (edited by P. N. Berkov), and the 1949 edition (edited by B. Ja. Buxštab). All editions since 1959 include the drama *Toržestvo dobrodeteli*. The best edition to date is the one by Buxštab in the "Biblioteka poeta" series: Koz'ma Prutkov, *Polnoe sobranie sočinenij* (Moscow–Leningrad, 1965). All my references to Prutkov's works and material concerning them, unless otherwise stated, are from this edition. The numerous editions, both scholarly and popular, since the Revolution have all had large press runs, the biggest being 225,000 copies in 1959. In contrast to this abundance, scholarship on Koz'ma Prutkov has been scant. Since the pioneering study by P. N. Berkov, *Koz'ma Prutkov, direktor probirnoj palatki i poet* (Leningrad–Moscow, 1933), there has appeared only one book-length work: I. A. Sukiasova, *Jazyk i stil' parodij Koz'my Prutkova* (Tbilisi, 1961). The best critical studies on Prutkov remain the articles and preface by Buxštab.

[2] The only translations have been made into two western Slavic languages, Slovak and Polish: Prutkov Kozma, *Z vol'ných chvil'* (Bratislava, 1961), and Prutkov Kozma, *Puch i pierze* (Warszawa, 1962).

[3] All dates will be given in the New Style.

working in an epoch of stern rule and prescribed thought, understood
the power of authority and command, and himself became an authority:
he does not earn, but demands respect, honor and even love, and—he
will receive it not only from his contemporaries but also from posterity."[4] Žemčužnikov echoes with good-natured facetiousness the self-
assurance of his creation. But the prophecy has held true. When in the
following year Pypin reviewed the newly-published *Complete Works of
Koz'ma Prutkov*, he gave a serious historical meaning to Prutkov's previous sporadic appearance in literary journals beginning in the first half of
the 1850's:

> The latest biographers and publishers of his works dwell little on the "histor-
> ical" meaning of his activity; but it is not without such meaning, and the
> historical conditions of the time in which Koz'ma Prutkov wrote explain
> sufficiently the success of his works and their very appearance. The beginning
> of the '50's may be counted as one of the especially difficult periods for Russian
> literature. It was a time of extraordinary constraints on science and litera-
> ture... All measures of strictness were put into play and a high secret censor-
> ship began to act in an extraordinary manner; the press avoided even the
> slightest shadow of live social thought or muffled it in a beclouded form of
> expression which would save it from suspicion, even though it caused the
> thought to be beclouded for the reader as well. People in whom social feelings
> were not silenced as well, to whom the interests of science and poetic creation
> were dear, saw themselves at a moral impasse. At that time Koz'ma Prutkov
> appeared, directed by his guardians... It was necessary somehow to entertain
> people in that state of apathy, of oppressive boredom and discontent from
> which there was no escape; an escape was found in laughter.[5]

In oppressive times, humor becomes of itself a kind of plea for innocence and a shield from reality. But, as we shall see, Tolstoj and the
Žemčužnikovs had other reasons, personal and literary, for inventing
Prutkov. They were the inheritors of the exuberant parodic wit of the
eighteenth century, when the men who shaped the language and the
literature of Russia developed their own style, in correcting through
parody the styles of their artistic peers. They also inherited the witty
epistolary tradition of the early part of their own century, when the cultured Russian reading public was even smaller than in their own day,
so that a poet's best friends were also his best audience. But if Koz'ma

---

[4] Koz'ma Prutkov, pp. 399-400.
[5] A. N. Pypin, "Polnoe sobranie sočinenij Koz'my Prutkova. SPb. 1884", *Vestnik
Evropy*, No. 3 (March, 1884), pp. 391-93. See also Sidney Monas, *The Third Section;
police and society in Russia under Nicholas I* (Cambridge: Harvard University Press,
1961).

Prutkov's sources were largely esoteric and his own origins indisputably aristocratic, his humor was of the broadest kind—preposterously illogical and obstreperously farcical—so that he had no trouble appealing to the journal-reading public in Russia.

Prutkov began as a sort of *mistifikacija*, in literary Russian an expansion of the pseudonym. In a literary mystification the author adopts not only the name but also the personality of the pseudo-author to whom his work is attributed. A mystification is intended to deceive the reader into accepting the reality of the pseudo-author and his pseudo-writings. In the case of Koz'ma Prutkov, however, the mystification was a transparent smoke-screen. While the exact identity of the authors remained unclear for decades, few people were ever deceived into believing that there really was a Koz'ma Prutkov. He has remained a universally acknowledged deception. Because of the collective nature of his creation, his name appears in most bibliographies of Russian authors, the only one to have achieved immortality without ever having lived.

The works of Koz'ma Prutkov contain both nonsense and parody. Often the line between the two is difficult to draw. Parody, the most in-bred form of literature, has always fed on other literature, giving an exaggerated imitation of it. It is the play of language upon language, literature upon literature. The peculiar pleasure that the reader or listener has always obtained from good parody comes from recognizing both its differences from and similarities to the work imitated. Marmontel defined the goal of parody in terms of this shock of recognition:

Le mérite et le but de la *parodie*, lorsqu'elle est bonne, est de faire sentir entre les plus grandes choses et les plus petites un rapport qui, par sa justesse et par sa nouveauté, nous cause une vive surprise: contraste et ressemblance, voilà les sources de la bonne plaisanterie; et c'est par-là que la *parodie* est ingénieuse et piquante.[6]

In ancient Greece parody became a legitimate genre, taking the epic as its source of inspiration. Parodies were included in festival contests from around 415 B.C. In these parodies the subject-matter but not the style of the epic was lowered.[7] Koz'ma Prutkov's writing includes parodies of epics in the epic style, but he also wrote in nearly all the genres which had proliferated in the modern age. There is another source of continuity between Koz'ma Prutkov and the ancients. Parody has always been a means of displaying wit. Quintilian at the end of Book Six of his

---

[6] J.-F. Marmontel, Eléments de littérature (Paris, 1787), p. 81.
[7] The main source of information on Greek parody is Athenaeus *Deipnosophists* xv.

Institutio Oratoria[8] mentions as a way of showing one's wit the invention of "verses resembling well-known lines, a trick styled parody by the
Greeks". Prutkov is only a would-be wit, and behind "his" parody
stands the real wit of his creators. Prutkov's bureaucratic-poetic personality (again we must return to the idea of the created personality in the
mystification) continually makes its imprint on the parody they write.

Pure parody, however, is relatively rare in Prutkov's works. Often
the parody contained in them is so broad that it has little or nothing to
do with any one author's work. Sometimes a whole tradition is imitated.
The plays are burlesques—parodies of entire genres like the vaudeville
or the mystery-play, with a broad, at times farcical humor. The fables
and much of the other poetry seems more like witty light verse than
witty parody of dull verse. Thus parody of an author is overshadowed
by parody of a genre and this in turn fades into humorous verse
written in that genre and using a particular style only as a point of
departure. This very generalized parody draws ever closer to pure
nonsense verse.

Parody may have either purely humorous or critical intentions toward
the work it imitates. In the latter case it resembles the censorious spirit
of satire. This kind of parody was, with few exceptions, alien to Prutkov's
works, for when they veer away from parody, it is usually not toward a
caricature of reality but towards verbal caricature, conjuring up a non-
sensical and absurd picture. G. K. Chesterton wrote, likening satire to
caricature:

> There is all the difference in the world between the instinct of satire, which,
> seeing in the Kaiser's moustaches something typical of him, draws them
> continually larger and larger; and the instinct of nonsense which, for no reason
> whatever, imagines what these moustaches would look like on the present
> Archbishop of Canterbury if he grew them in a fit of absence of mind.[9]

Tolstoj and the Žemčužnikovs took a real enough personage, the Russian
bureaucrat, but they attributed to him a wildly improbable body of
writing which often parodied other Russian poets. Their brand of non-
sense-parody brushes against reality at times, but more often creates a
new, humorous order of reality quite distinct from any invented before
or since. The works of Koz'ma Prutkov are among the greatest purely
humorous works of Russian literature.

---

[8] Quintilian *Institutio Oratoria* vi. 3. 96-97.
[9] G. K. Chesterton, *The Defendant* (New York: Dodd, Mead and Co., 1906), p. 44.

I

THE INVENTORS OF KOZ'MA PRUTKOV

Ce qu'il y a d'enivrant dans le mauvais goût, c'est le
plaisir aristocratique de déplaire.
— Charles Baudelaire

It is not difficult to see that Aleksej Tolstoj and the Žemčužnikov brothers
(Aleksej, Aleksandr and Vladimir) had much in common, much that
would enable them to write together: kinship, physical proximity on
their estates and in Petersburg, an excellent education, a reluctant familiarity with the world of officialdom, an involvement in the Russian literary world yet a certain aristocratic aloofness from its quarrels—and,
above all, a respect for excellence in literary creation combined with a
sense of the ridiculous in art as well as in life. Koz'ma Prutkov was the
child of their carefree youth, and like many children he became the
opposite of his parents as much as possible. But there must also have
been some special reason, one more thing they had in common, which
caused Tolstoj and the Žemčužnikovs to create the exact personage they
did. Humor can take many forms, but the cousins settled upon one in
particular.

In a letter to A. N. Pypin, Vladimir Žemčužnikov quotes a letter from
his brother Aleksej answering some questions about Koz'ma Prutkov.
Aleksej said that:

Although each of us had his special political character, one common trait
closely united us all: the complete absence of "bureaucratism" (kazennost')
in ourselves and consequently a great sensitivity to everything bureaucratic.
This trait helped us—at first independently of our will and completely unpremeditatedly—to create the type of Koz'ma Prutkov, who is bureaucratic to
such an extent that not a single "burning question" of the day reaches his
thought or feeling if not from a bureaucratic point of view. He is funny because
he is completely guiltless. He seems to say in his works, "everything human is
alien to me." ... We richly endowed Prutkov with those qualities which made

him a man useless *(nenužnyj)* for these times, and mercilessly removed those qualities which could have made him even a little useful for his epoch. The absence of the latter of these qualities and the presence of the former are equally comic.[1]

Russian literature has as one of its obsessive themes the description of the educated Russian, sincerely concerned with the problems of his country, yet somehow feeling himself incapable of helping to solve them. Two members of the Prutkovian triumvirate attempted government work, but found it futile and frustrating. As writers, Tolstoj's preoccupation with historical events and Žemčužnikov's with "civic" themes coexisted, as we shall see, with a natural tendency to withdraw into the self-contained world of the perfectly-polished love or nature lyric. Somewhere amdist this artistic duality there arose "at first independently of our will and completely unpremeditatedly" a character who would incarnate a humorous solution to dilemmas that were not theirs alone, a personage whose views were consistent where a liberal but uncommitted man saw little opportunity for consistency. Prutkov treads fearlessly through nineteenth-century Russian reality; he has an answer for the cursed questions. An easy answer can only appear humorous to men who have found none. The fact that Žemčužnikov speaks of Prutkov in terms of usefulness shows a concern of his own, not of Prutkov's. Prutkov has lost the fear of being unnecessary; his creators obviously had not.

Unlike his creators, Prutkov has totally vanquished any fear of smugness. A completely smug man would never ask himself if he were necessary or ridiculous to those around him. Men who came to maturity in the self-contained world of the aristocracy, abundantly endowed with native talent as well, would, if they were at all sensitive, be extremely aware of the peril of becoming too self-satisfied. One critic has made just this point:

In the delicate mind of the cultured Russian there dwells a fear of self-satisfaction. And that very trait gives breadth to Russian satire. That characteristic gave birth to Koz'ma Prutkov. Is it not noteworthy that one of the authors of Koz'ma Prutkov was the gentle, sensitive, excellent Count Aleksej Tolstoj?[2]

The Russian nobleman, immune to all other social ills, was still prone to ridicule. When Žemčužnikov wrote that "one common trait closely

[1]   Koz'ma Prutkov, p. 393. The quotation is a backward echo of Terence's "Humani nihil a me alienum puto" (*Heauton Timorumenos* I. i. 25).
[2]   Homo Novus A. P. Kugel', "Zametki", *Teatr i iskusstvo*, No. 3 (1913), p. 68.

united us all: the complete absence of bureaucratism in ourselves and consequently a great sensitivity to anything bureaucratic", he is protesting too much. People are generally most sensitive to what is close to them. It is more likely that the cousins were so sensitive to the official world because they saw it permanently rooted in their country; a world as smug and self-contained as their own, but substituting aimless activity for aimless inactivity. Furthermore, as we shall see, in practice the two worlds overlapped. Many of the gentry became civil servants or did military service (or both: it was easy to move from one to the other since they had an equivalent system of ranks) for at least part of their lives; and conversely, almost the entire civil service was staffed by members of the gentry. Thus the terms "aristocrat" and "bureaucrat" refer not to two different classes as much as to two different sets of values and attitudes to government and life. When the aristocrat found himself in both worlds at once, he felt his integrity compromised and his creativity stifled. His dignity slipped from him into the hands of the State. His free creative talents were harnessed to the machinery of state documents. His spontaneous right to laugh at others and himself was threatened by the morbid seriousness of officialdom. The aristocrat feared nothing more than becoming like the official, not because he was less well-groomed and less cultured (they could never become either), but because the official was blithely unaware of being ridiculous.

Prutkov was not an enemy to be demolished by the heavy weapon of satire; his creators had a genuine affection for him. Having invented him, they were free of him.[3] They could indulge any penchant for literary triviality and sentential aphorizing of their own without being accused of it. "He is funny because he is completely guiltless" were the wisest words ever written about Prutkov. Under his name, the men who created him could partake of that same, rare guiltlessness.

The lives and works of Prutkov's creators were somewhat eclipsed by the glory of their creation. Only Aleksej Tolstoj maintained a separate literary reputation throughout his life; and it may be repeated with certainty that to most Russians "Junker Šmidt is better known than the monologue of Fedor Ioannovič."[4] While a casual reader can take

---

[3] To use the terminology of Kenneth Burke, Koz'ma Prutkov was a strategy of his creators, equipping them with the impiety of the ridiculous against an enemy they found oppressive. See especially *The Philosophy of Literary Form* (New York: Random House, 1957). Of course, the enemy can be within the author as well as outside him.

[4] Koz'ma Prutkov, *Proizvedenija ne vošedšie v sobranie sočinenij*, ed. P. K. Guber (Petrograd–Moscow, 1923), p. 5.

Koz'ma Prutkov at face value, the literary historian, by examining separately the biographies of the men who wrote under the name of Prutkov, can begin to determine why these men invented this particular character and what gave them such unity of style and purpose.[5]

Aleksej Tolstoj and the Žemčužnikov brothers put into the character of Koz'ma Prutkov traits which both amused and frightened them. From a distance the bureaucratic world looked ridiculously self-inflated, but at closer range its grotesque proportions became nightmarish. The noble Russian was often forced to come closer. He enjoyed wealth, education and family pride, but not immunity from the bureaucracy. Occasionally he was its prey or its victim, but more often he simply found himself a part of it.

A true aristocrat and a genuine poet, Aleksej Tolstoj (1817–1875) had difficulty in disengaging himself from the Prutkovian dilemma of leading a double life. Brjullov's portrait of Tolstoj, painted in 1836, shows a handsome youth with features totally unlike Prutkov's—blond hair, large blue eyes and an expression quietly noble and sensitive. In the forties Tolstoj led the typical life of society youth, enjoying good looks and physical strength. But he was also a civil servant. When he had passed his university examinations, a certificate was issued to him, giving him the right to serve in the government as an official of moderately high rank. In the late thirties, after a short period of service with the Department of Economic Affairs in Saint Petersburg, he became attached to the Russian Embassy in Frankfurt. In 1840 he returned to Russia where promotions followed nearly every year: in 1842 he became titular councillor, in 1843 "page of the chamber of His Majesty", in 1845 collegiate assessor, and in 1846 councillor of the court.

By 1851, within a year of the time Koz'ma Prutkov was created, Tolstoj had become fully aware that he was being forced to take a path he was more than reluctant to follow. In a letter of October 14 to his future wife Sof'ja Andreevna Miller he writes:

---

[5] For the distinction between the biography of poets in the reader's consciousness and the necessity of biographical calculation by the historian of literature, see B.. Tomaševskij, *Literatura i biografija* (Moscow, 1923), pp. 6-9. André Breton makes a more direct and rather interesting challenge to the critic: "...je trouve souhaitable que la critique, renonçant, il est vrai, à ses plus chères prérogatives, mais se proposant à tout prendre, un but moins vain que celui de la mise au point toute mécanique des idées, se borne à de savantes incursions dans le domaine qu'elle se croit le plus interdit et qui est, en dehors de l'oeuvre, celui où la personne de l'auteur, en proie aux menus faits de la vie courante, s'exprime en toute indépendance, d'une manière souvent si distinctive." André Breton, *Nadja* (Paris: Gallimard, 1964), pp. 11-12.

...You cannot imagine with what pleasure I see people who have devoted themselves to any art whatsoever.

To see people over fifty, who have lived and live in the name of art and who treat it seriously always gives me great pleasure because it is such a sharp difference from the so-called "service" and from all people, who, under the pretext that they serve, live by intrigues one filthier than the next. ...

I do not wish to speak of myself now, but sometime I will tell you how little I am born for an official life and how little benefit I can bring to it.

I was born an artist, but all circumstances and all my life until now have prevented me from becoming *completely* an artist.

In general, our whole administration and general structure is the downright enemy of everything artistic—from poetry to the construction of streets.[6]

Tolstoj tells Sof'ja Andreevna that his real vocation is to be a writer. Not until ten years and several promotions later did an "imperial ruling" finally grant Tolstoj his retirement "for domestic reasons". His letter of resignation, sent to the Tsar on September 28, 1861, shows both tact and conviction:

Longtemps j'ai pensé a la manière dont je devrais parler à Votre Majesté d'un sujet qui me tient à coeur, et je suis arrivé à la conviction que le chemin droit en ceci est le meilleur, comme en toute chose. Sire, le service, *quel qu'il soit*, est profondement contraire à ma nature; je sais que chacun doit, selon le degré de ses forces, être utile à son pays, mais il y a différentes manières d'être utile. Celle qui m'a été désignée par la Providence, c'est mon talent litté-raire, et toute autre voie m'est impossible. Je serai toujours un mauvais officier et un mauvais employé, mais je crois pouvoir dire sans présomption, Sire, que je suis un bon écrivain. Cette vocation n'est pas nouvelle en moi; je l'aurais suivie depuis longtemps si je n'avais pas cru devoir, pendant un certain temps, me faire violence (jusqu'à l'âge de quarante ans), par égard pour mes parents qui avaient une manière de voir contraire à la mienne. ... Je croyais alors pouvoir vaincre ma nature qui est toute artistique, mais l'expérience m'a prouvé que je lutterais en vain contre elle. *Le service et l'art sont incompatibles*, l'un nuit à l'autre, et il faut choisir entre les deux.[7]

Tolstoj's conviction about the incompatibility of government service and art gave birth to Prutkov, whose credo was the opposite, who believed that service in the bureaucrary came first and that art followed naturally. Tolstoj expelled the demon that had haunted his own life by giving it a name, a personality, and a literary activity that assumed the name of art. He could then proceed to mock all the literary schools of the present and previous age to which he felt no kinship whatsoever.

[6] A. K. Tolstoj, *Sobranie sočinenij* (Moscow, 1964), IV, 52-53.
[7] André Lirondelle, *Le poète Alexis Tolstoi, l'homme et l'oeuvre* (Paris: Hachette, 1912), pp. 192-93.

Tolstoj found it difficult to infuse his poetry with an ideology and avoided close connections with any of the literary groups. On June 18, 1857, he wrote to Sof'ja Andreevna: "I will not be pleased if you make the acquaintance of Nekrasov. Our paths are different."[8] And although he revelled in the Slavophiles' praise of his poetry,[9] he was far from becoming their literary spokesman. Koz'ma Prutkov wrote Slavophile poetry. Tolstoj himself wrote poetry against the radicals (for example, "Protiv tečenija" or "Poroj veseloj maja") and against the conservative hierarchy (as in the poem which begins: "Sidit pod baldaxinom/Kitaec Cu-Kin-Cyn"). The former he depicted as base destroyers of beauty; the latter as what the Chinese name means in Russian.[10]

Tolstoj's penchant for humor had displayed itself long before 1850 and continued throughout his creative life. He is the only one of Prutkov's creators whose humorous works form a significant part of his own writings. Tolstoj's humorous poetry cannot be separated from his serious lyrics on any formal basis. In all his shorter works, including those written for Prutkov, Tolstoj preferred four-line stanzas, consisting of iambic verse and with cross-rhyme. Tolstoj's only formal innovation is his use of new and unusual rhymes, one of the most important devices of humorous poetry generally; this may well help explain why light verse came easily to him.

His letters, like that of May 9, 1869 to Markevič,[11] crackle with polylinguistic puns. He carried on a regular correspondence with the historian N. I. Kostomarov in a somewhat Russianized Old Church Slavonic.[12] We may assume that much of Tolstoj's written humor has been lost, misplaced, or thrown out with the same nonchalance with which it was produced. Just as the creation of the personage Prutkov had as a side effect the preserving of light verse written in the spirit of a moment, so their incorporation into letters preserved many of Tolstoj's other literary witticisms.

Tolstoj's letters to N. V. Adlerberg, a young officer, written in 1837–1838,[13] accompanied by sketches, contain much of Prutkov *avant la lettre*, although their rather formless exuberance might discourage a literary audience: they contain playlets with some of Tolstoj's favorite

[8] Tolstoj, IV, 95.
[9] See the letter of September 7, 1856 to Sof'ja Andreevna, *ibid.*, p. 83.
[10] *I.e.*, S.O.B.
[11] See Lirondelle, p. 524ff, for the original French.
[12] Tolstoj, IV, 196-97 and 327-28.
[13] *Ibid.*, pp. 457-519.

macaronic language, they are full of suggestively absurd names (e.g., a lady named Manufaktura), *non sequiturs* in dialogue, ditties in lofty diction, and parody (including an excellent one of a gypsy song in a fantasy entitled "Floran Tailleur; Viktor Portnoj"). But in general these letters prove that alogic by itself loses its impact when it lacks the logic of a formal structure to contain it. Characters in a play must have some motive for their behavior, but here Tolstoj mocks the rule that "il ne faut rien faire qui ne soit motivé."[14] Most interesting of all is that Tolstoj expected his friend Adlerberg to cooperate and embellish the joke himself. "I have given you the idea, kindly develop it yourself",[15] he says at one point. But whether or not the young officer had the collaborative talents of the Žemčužnikovs is unknown, for his side of the correspondence has been lost.

Two prose fables written at the end of the 1830's further attest to Tolstoj's humorous talents at the beginning of his career. They may also be considered early attempts at a comic narrative or *skaz* form. In the "Fable of How One Philosopher was Left without Cucumbers", the style of narration has the simplicity of a fairy tale, and is full of conversational interjections and self-corrections ("when autumn came, that is, not autumn, but spring..."[16]). While this fable is based largely on Krylov, the fable "How the Young President Washington Made Himself A Man in A Short Time"[17] is based primarily on Tolstoj's imaginary historical *non sequiturs* and puns. The young Washington buys a cat for 300,000,000 million and goes to America. He rids the continent of mice and shaves the natives, who have extremely heavy beards. The Inca *(sic)* is so grateful that he grants the wish of Washington who asks to be made President of the United States. Back at the Alhambra *(sic)* he receives the name of Washington Irving. Irving is an abbreviation for "Inke Rezal Volosy Inostrannyj Negociant Georgij" ("the foreign merchant George cut the hair of the Inca"). This neat little anecdote is somewhat similar in anti-historicity to Prutkov's "Historical Materials", except that the type of narrator is entirely different. Here we have the simple story-teller instead of the pretentious, if equally simple, pseudo-historian.

It is tempting to fall into the conclusion that because Tolstoj was the most talented writer of the Prutkov collaborators and because his humor was fully displayed in numerous other works, he contributed more or

---

[14] *Ibid.*, p. 515.
[15] *Ibid.*, p. 472.
[16] Tolstoj, III, 551.
[17] *Ibid.*, pp. 555-58.

better works to the Prutkov effort.[18] One may make several objections to this argument, two of which must now be considered. First, one of the chief marvels of the Prutkov collaboration remains its unity of style, so that stylistically it is largely impossible to differentiate works in order to ascribe them to a particular author.

Secondly, even the Prutkovian works definitely written by Tolstoj (i.e., those ascribed to him by the Žemčužnikov brothers or by himself) have a style markedly different from his three greatest humorous creations—"The Rebellion in the Vatican", "The History of the Russian State from Gostomysl to Timašev", and "The Dream of Popov".[19] The *risqué* humor of the first, a tale of how the eunuchs rebelled against the Pope, with a "variant for the ladies" when the language becomes unprintable, is quite like that of Puškin's *Gavriliada*, but far removed from the usual propriety of Prutkov. The "History of the Russian State", written in 1868, parodies Russian history by selecting a theme from Nestor's Chronicle "Vsja zemlja naša velika i obilna, a narjada v nej net" ("all our land is great and abundant, but there is no order in it") and repeating it with variations throughout as the Russians try repeatedly to bring order to their rich land. The Varangians speak German presumably just for local color, and even Vladimir's reign is summed up succinctly in the verse:

Когда ж вступил Владимир	When Vladimir ascended
На свой отцовский трон,	the paternal throne
Da endigte für immer	there ended forever
Die alte Religion	the old religion.

The poem, composed of eighty-three such quatrains, derives its humor from the cumulative effect of a series of witty résumés of Russian historical events. The satirical analogy, that Russia's past troubles resemble

---

[18] The authors of the two full-length books on Koz'ma Prutkov both try to give Tolstoj pre-eminence. I. M. Sukiasova repeatedly attempts to ascribe works to Tolstoj when the authorship is in doubt. She states further that because the Žemčužnikovs were lesser writers, they could not have written Prutkov's better works. See her *Jazyk i stil' parodij Koz'my Prutkova*, pp. 60, 73, 213. P. N. Berkov admits that "the central figure among the creators of Prutkov was V. M. Žemčužnikov", but he still insists that "to Aleksej Tolstoj belong the most artistic pieces of Prutkov". He does not, however, explain what he means by "artistic" (xudožestvennye). See Koz'ma Prutkov, *Polnoe sobranie sočinenija*, ed. P. N. Berkov (Moscow–Leningrad: Academia, 1933), p. 595. For a further example of this argument, see L. B. Modzalevskij, "Koz'ma Prutkov i Aleksej Tolstoj," *Krasnaja Nov'*, No. 4 (1926), pp. 107-11.

[19] These and all the other short verses to follow in this chapter are quoted according to Tolstoj, Vol. I.

her present ones, is obvious. Tolstoj is writing here *in propria persona*,
and he even signs his name in the last couplet:

Составил от былинок	Composed from old tales
Рассказ немудрый сей	Was this foolish story
Худый смиренный инок,	By the unworthy humble monk
Раб божий Алексей.	God's servant Aleksej.

The whole tone of the poem rings with sophisticated good-humored
sarcasm, hardly a tone that Prutkov would employ.

The Dream of Popov has been compared by nearly every Prutkovian
commentator to Prutkov himself, for the obvious reason that it tells the
tale of a bureaucrat. But this mature and masterful satire, written in
1873—long after Tolstoj had ceased contribution to Prutkov—has more
differences than similarities to the light humor of Prutkov. Being a satire,
it is tied to reality, a political and social reality which intervenes quite
differently in the absurd fancies of Prutkov. The hero Tit Evseič Popov
is a timid bureaucrat; when he dreams he has appeared at a reception
in honor of his minister's name-day correctly dressed but without his
pants, his dream becomes a real nightmare. The minister who in a
"liberal" speech has been calling himself a servant of the people becomes
infuriated at poor Tit, "and the minister was still more gorgeous (kraše)
in anger than in kindness", says the narrator ironically. The Third Section, where Tit is taken, tries first paternalism ("Oh youth!" he says,
although, as the narrator reminds us, Popov was over forty), then threats
on Tit (at one point calling him a "haughty *sans-culotte*"). Popov, in his
fright, is led to denounce all his friends. The narrator concludes "how
people in terror are vile". At this point Popov awakens. Prutkov, for all
his bureaucratic soul, is never faced with such deeply motivated, psycho-
logically tormented moments of bureaucratic reality. In a world of
wolves and sheep, he is more the aggressor than the victim, but his acti-
vities are harmless. Most important, in *The Dream of Popov* the narrator
continually makes ironic asides. This narrator, obviously close to Tolstoj
himself, concludes the poem by denying that such a situation could
occur in Russia and claims, with the Gogolian ironic disclaimer: "I am
not responsible for the dreams of others." In the works of Prutkov, the
tutors need not interject their own voices. Indeed, they make a point of
standing far away from their creation and letting him speak for himself.
There is no harsh reality to affirm by denial, as in *Popov*, for reality has
disappeared from view altogether. The works of Prutkov resemble the
appearance of Tit Evseič at the grand reception. Everything is in perfect

order, except that one crucial thing is missing; the poems and plays, unlike Tolstoj's satires, are for the most part not meant to be taken seriously.

Therefore if any comparison between Tolstoj the humorist and Tolstoj the Prutkovian can be made, it must be found not in the most important of his humorous works but, as we have seen, in his letters and in the occasional poems, the spontaneous parodies. These most personal of Tolstoj's writings were composed not for publication but for the delight of friend, or sometimes merely for self-amusement. The short cycle of "Medical Poems" had as its hero the doctor A. S. Krivskij, who served at Tolstoj's estate Krasnyj Rog from 1868 to 1870. They poke light fun at the freethinking doctor and were doubtless written to tease him. In one of them, for instance, a sexton tells the doctor that amber is formed from hard-boiled eggs in the stomach. The doctor, "of a skeptical frame of mind/Did not love persons of the Church" and swallows five hundred eggs and dies, while the sexton triumphantly reiterates his theory.

An even more personal poem, written to A. M. Žemčužnikov in 1854, begins "Vxožu v tvoj kabinet" and is just a note in verse form inviting his cousin to lunch. He enumerates what the menu will be and ends with a Prutkovian touch:

Армянский славный край	The wonderful land of Armenia
Лежит за Араратом,	Lies beyond the Ararat,
Пожалуй приезжай	Please come and see
Ко мне сегодня с братом!	Me today with your brother!

A final source for Prutkov can be found in Tolstoj's jottings in his books. He wrote epigraphs in verse to Puškin's poems, sometimes expressing admiration, but more often poking fun at his great predecessor. Some of the verses parody Puškin's style. For example, in the margins of the poem "Želanije", Tolstoj could not resist mocking Puškin's overuse of figures and props from antiquity, with concomitant notions of idleness and careless bliss.

Вакх, Лель, хариты, томны урны,
Проказники, повесы, шалуны,
Цевницы, лиры, лень, Авзонии сыны,
Камены, музы, грации лазурны,
Питомцы, баловни луны,
Наперсники пиров, любимцы Цитереи
И прочие небрежные лакеи.

Bacchus, Lel', Charites, languid urns,
Mischief-makers, rakes, imps,
Reed-pipes, lyres, idleness, sons of Ausonias,
Camenae, muses, azure graces,
Nurselings, minions of the moon,
Confidants of feasts, favorites of Cytherea
And other careless lackeys.

The epithets are so decorative that they often have nothing to do with the noun they modify.

All these poems lack to make them truly Prutkovian is a purposeful clumsiness. Tolstoj's voice can still be heard in the last line of the Puškin parody, making the final witty point. The medical poems too let the "superior" voice of the author be heard. With Prutkov, Tolstoj would find a voice so extravagantly comic that he and his cousins could lose their own and let their creation speak for himself. For Tolstoj's own artistic development, Prutkov represented the true perfection of his considerable talent for light verse.

Unlike their cousin, the Žemčužnikov brothers were not humorists in their own right. Indeed, only one of them was a writer at all. But they had exactly the same background as Tolstoj: one in which poetry, whether in a cast-away album or better in a hastily-written script for a family playlet, casually flourished and was lost. Even if we did not have proof that they wrote most of Prutkov's works, it would be foolish to say they could not have written them because they wrote no other great or lasting comic work. But textual proof does exist that Vladimir (1830–1884) and Aleksej (1821–1908) Žemčužnikov wrote the largest part of Koz'ma Prutkov, and that a third brother, Aleksandr (1826–1896), made enthusiastic if limited contributions of his own.

The oldest of the Žemčužnikov brothers, Aleksej, like his cousin Tolstoj, held high official posts, yet abandoned the civil service permanently in 1858. In some verses of 1844 he writes of how he lived "like a mouse, in layers of archival dust",[20] adding that:

If hell await me beyond the tomb, —
I make one, one plea alone:
That my spirit not be shut in the Senate, —
All other tortures I will bear.[21]

---

[20]   A. M. Žemčužnikov, *Izbrannye proizvedenija* (Moscow–Leningrad, 1963), p. 261.
[21]   *Ibid.*

He devoted his long life to writing poetry distinctly inferior to that of his cousin.[22] He began to write most of his work in the 1870's, long after the time of Koz'ma Prutkov, and then wrote political or philosophical poems and nature or love lyrics. He was especially well known for his "civic" poetry. At the time of the Crimean War he wrote an extremely patriotic poem "To the Russians", quite the opposite of Prutkov's military aphorisms, but he later excluded this poem from his collected works. He also wrote satires, serious in tone and lacking Tolstoj's wit. Indeed, one could almost be cruel enough to apply some of Prutkov's parodies to Aleksej Žemčužnikov's lyrics. Nevertheless, Žemčužnikov's greatest weakness was sentimentality, not Prutkovian pomposity. He was especially sentimental about old age and about Russia as in the poem "Testament" written in 1897:

> My last strength is going,
> I have done what I could; I can do no more.
> I stand in debt before my country still
> But may she forgive me at the grave's edge.[23]

Aleksej Žemčužnikov's "Autobiographical Sketch" written in 1892 gives us a few interesting clues to his character. He divides his life into two periods: before and after his retirement of 1858. Only the second half does he take seriously, only then does he claim to begin to think for himself. His period of service he remembered as a time of unrelieved gloom. Like Tolstoj, he does not take sides in art. He apologizes for not writing much poetry on civic themes, claiming with extreme modesty that Nekrasov was doing this so well that it would have been useless to repeat him (or did writing civic poetry become more of a duty than a need at times?). "On the other hand, so-called 'pure' poetry, aloof from the news of the day, is always lofty and beautiful. A time when it would seem unnecessary could not be."[24] Žemčužnikov's sympathy with all kinds of poetry, provided it is poetry, is part of a *largesse d'esprit* which made it possible for him to contribute to Prutkov as much as he did. A bitter enemy of one or another of the current literary camps could never have the range of targets that Žemčužnikov hit with Prutkov, nor the gentle subtlety with which he made his mark.

When the time of Prutkov was long past, Žemčužnikov wanted to be

---

[22]   For a sympathetic and extensive review of his poetry, see N. I. Ammon, "Polveka poetičeskogo služenija", *Russkaja mysl'*, IX (1901), 172-203.

[23]   Žemčužnikov, p. 215.

[24]   *Ibid.*, p. 65.

remembered only as a serious poet. He never mentions Prutkov in his
"Autobiographical Sketch" except to refer to him once as "the popular
Koz'ma Prutkov". He adds, "I never was popular."[25] Žemčužnikov's
own collected works were published at the same time as one of the
numerous editions of Prutkov. In the following year (1893) he wrote
with some bitterness to M. M. Stasjulevič: "I may observe that the works
of Prutkov sell much better than my verses."[26]

Aleksej Žemčužnikov speaks to posterity mainly as an old man, and
old men tend to reject their youth. Koz'ma Prutkov was the best work
of his youth, but not his only attempt at humor. One of the best of
Žemčužnikov's society verses "In the Album of N. N.", dated November
28, 1853, was canonized only thirty years later, in the first edition of
Prutkov's *Complete Works*. Not written expressly for Prutkov, it is still
worthy of him. It makes the metaphorical "serpent of melancholy" into
a real snake by cutting it in half in a sort of comic *realizacija metafory*.
When the poet writes his verse for the young lady's album, he tears half a
page from his own diary and pastes it into her album, leaving half of
his serpent of melancholy in either place:

Желанья вашего всегда покорный раб,
Из книги дней моих я вырву полстраницы
И в ваш альбом вклею... Вы знаете, я слаб
Пред волей женщины, тем более девицы.
Вклею!.. Но вижу я, уж вас объемлет страх!
Змеей тоски моей пришлось мне поделиться;
Не целая змея теперь во мне, но — ах! —
Зато по ползмеи в обоих шевелится.

Ever your humble servant when you speak,
Out of my diary half a page I tear
And paste it in your book... You know I'm weak
Before the will of woman, the more so maiden fair.
I paste it in!... But now you tremble so!
Of my heart's serpent now you do partake;
Now not one serpent lies in me but—oh! —
In each of us there wriggles half a snake.

Much of his light verse, *poésie fugitive*, and comedy was never published,
but some manuscripts survive.[27] They reveal occasional poems, "jokes",

[25] *Ibid.*, p. 66.
[26] Koz'ma Prutkov, ed. P. N. Berkov, p. 490.
[27] In CGALI, Arxiv A. M. Žemčužnikova, Fond 639, opis' 1 and in the BiL. Ruko-
pisnij otdel, muzejnoe sobranie, Fond 101, No. 4808; Fond 178, Nos. 4806, 5283.

and four comedies of the early 1850's with very little real wit or humor; but they also show that Žemčužnikov was impressed by Musset's *Proverbes*, Griboedov, and Lermontov. The comedy *The Strange Night (Strannaja noč')* illustrates the quasi-proverb "there are women with heart and brains, but none without coquetry".[28] *A Wedding for a Wedding (Svad'ba dlja svad'by)* has a specifically Russian setting: the local color of a fair. *Demjan Konstantinovič Prokof'ev is in need of a wife and money* and *The Madman (Sumasšedšij*—influenced by Griboedov's *Woe from Wit)* seem artificial and far from anything Prutkovian. Žemčužnikov did well to let these works lie forgotten. They are of interest to us only because they show that, *in propria persona*, Žemčužnikov wrote no play worthy of Prutkov. But, writing alone in September 1883, he would produce for Prutkov's collected works an excellent mystery-play, *The Affinity of Universal Forces*. His humor had matured and became refined, even though it was rarely exercised in those years. When he guided Prutkov's pen, Žemčužnikov wrote his best works.

Aleksandr Žemčužnikov collaborated in the writing of three fables and two plays for Prutkov, and wrote some smaller works on his own. He seems to have been the ringleader in the various pranks and practical jokes for which the Žemčužnikovs were remembered in various memoirs.[29] The anecdotes may have been exaggerated as they were passed around town, but they all have as a *leitmotiv* the persecution of some high-ranking personage. Aleksandr would deliberately step on the foot of an important bureaucrat and then come to him at every reception with profuse apologies.[30] Or, dressed in uniform, he would go around at night telling various architects to appear at court on the following day because St. Isaac's Cathedral had collapsed. Or, when he found that a certain minister of finances would take a walk in a certain place at ten o'clock every morning, he would stroll by, greeting him with the words "the minister of finances is the mainspring of activity". Aping the manners of officialdom was a favorite Žemčužnikov habit long before Prutkov, their most memorable practical joke, came into being. Aleksandr also joked in writing, but his brother Vladimir dealt rather severely

[28] A. M. Žemčužnikov, *Sočinenija v dvux tomax* (St. Petersburg, 1898), Vol. II.
[29] See: N. A. Kotljarevskij, *Starinnye portrety* (St. Petersburg, 1907), pp. 411-13; P. K. Mart'janov, *Dela i ljudi veka* (St. Petersburg, 1896), III, 238-39; V. P. Meščerskij, *Moi vospominanija* (St. Petersburg, 1897), I, 94-95; L. M. Žemčužnikov, *Moi vospominanija iz prošlogo* (Leningrad, 1926), p. 80.
[30] Cf. Čexov's early story "Smert' činovnika" in which a minor official (here inadvertently) sneezes upon an important personage and literally dies of apologizing.

with most of his work, not deeming it right for Prutkov. More than once Aleksandr published on his own under the name of Prutkov. He was not the only one who did this, but in *Iskra (The Spark)* in 1861 and 1862 there appeared a series of works signed by Prutkov, some of which were probably written by Aleksandr. This may have led the other brothers to declare Prutkov dead in 1863. Undismayed, Aleksandr continued to publish in *St.-Petersburgskie vedomosti (The St. Petersburg News)* of 1876 notes "from the other world", biographical materials, unpublished aphorisms and verse of Prutkov; in the 1870's, he was the only one of Prutkov's creators who published at all. Although Vladimir included very little of Aleksandr's material in the *Complete Works*, subsequent editors have not excluded him entirely from the Prutkovian canon, for his works have a charm of their own.

Vladimir, however, was more interested in preserving an "authentic" Koz'ma Prutkov. In March 1884 he wrote to a relative, V. B. Perovskaja, who had apparently asked why *Ljubov' and Silin*, a play by Aleksandr, had not been included in the Complete Works. Vladimir answered: "*Ljubov' and Silin* was printed by brother Aleksandr in the name of K. Prutkov, without the knowledge and approval of the others; in it there is something humorous, largely taken from jokes known previously in our family; but for Prutkov the merely humorous is not sufficient—there must also be a literary finish and a certain kind of humor."[31] Vladimir maintains that Aleksandr wrote in his own way when he was on his own and only by collaboration with himself or Aleksej did he write in a Prutkovian style. As for possible revision of Aleksandr's works, "we both felt heavy, old, especially when we are not together."[32] Koz'ma Prutkov represented a consistent collaborative effort and a certain standard of literary polish. While he may not have been right in excluding a few of Aleksandr's works, including the play in question, Vladimir Žemčužnikov generally had unerring vision in both his capacaties, as editor and as author of Prutkov. Were it not for him, Koz'ma Prutkov might be a mere *nom de plume* among many others in the journals of the time.

Vladimir Žemčužnikov, the youngest brother was still a student at the University in Petersburg when Koz'ma Prutkov was created. (Aleksandr had just finished university and the elder cousins were already in government service at the time.) In 1854, when Vladimir completed his education, he went to Tobolsk to serve under a relative who was governor

---

[31] Koz'ma Prutkov, p. 452.
[32] *Ibid.*, p. 453.

there. Next year he joined the army, serving until 1857; later he became a Director of the Russian Society of Shipping and Trade. After that he never remained long in any one ministry, but continued to work all his life in important government posts. From his many changes of position, we may assume that his sense of duty was matched by his dissatisfaction with each office and ministry which he came to know. Unlike his cousin or brother, he did not consider himself a literary figure and wrote nothing except his contributions for Prutkov. Paradoxically, not only did he write more of Prutkov than anyone else, but also, as has been noted, he prepared the *Complete Works*, indicated authorship for separate works, and wrote the "Biographical facts". As early as 1853 he had begun, with the approval of the others, to edit Prutkov's works, but he fulfilled this task only in 1884, nine years after Aleksej Tolstoj's death and a few months before his own. As both his letters and his late Prutkovian writings show, he retained more than enough talent and wit to codify and canonize Prutkov forever. As he wrote to Pypin in 1885, "I loved Koz'ma Petrovič Prutkov very much and therefore I say decisively that he was a genius."[33] Vladimir had the good sense and the good taste to recognize Prutkov's worth, and the modesty to let Prutkov take all the laurels. In all his writings there is the same delightful hint of self-mockery for having the unique opportunity to praise his own creation without being accused of self-praise.

Vladimir wrote most of the works for which Prutkov is largely famous—the parodies. Perhaps the fact that he was not himself a writer, but very much a cultivated man of letters, caused him to look dispassionately upon the weaknesses of others who attempted, more or less successfully, to write. In any case, Vladimir, like the others, knew most of the literary figures of the day, from Chernyševskij to writers of lyrics. Very little of Russia's literary past or present must have escaped his critical eye.

These were the inventors of Koz'ma Prutkov. Taking an aristocratic pleasure in displeasing, they were themselves intoxicated with the vulgarity of their creation.

[33]   *Ibid.*, p. 400.

II

PRUTKOV FROM CREATION TO CANONIZATION

Tolstoj and the Žemčužnikovs liked to call themselves Prutkov's "guardians" and their solicitous presence was essential at all stages of Prutkov's
genesis and literary career—his birth, his naming, his appearance in the
journals of the time, and his canonization in the *Complete Works*. Koz'ma
Prutkov came to life gradually. It took not only a general exuberance on
the part of his creators, but also several purposeful collaborative literary
efforts before the idea of creating a special pseudonym occurred to anyone. His works appeared both on stage and in print before Prutkov
emerged as their author.

Aleksej Žemčužnikov gave an interview to the *Peterburgskaya gazeta
(The Petersburg Gazette)* in 1896 in which he related the following:

We were then very young, healthy, merry, without cares and lived well,
thank God, without any sorrow. So we thought, my cousin Count Aleksej
Tolstoj and I, of writing a comic playlet entitled *Fantasia*. We wrote in one
room, on separate tables. We divided the play into an even number of scenes.
He took one part for himself and I took the other. When we finished working
and joined both parts, it happened that in one part the actors left the stage,
and in the other they entered. There was no link between them. . . . We laughed
until we cried about our creation. Then we thought up a middle part. We put
into the play thunder, a storm, etc., and gave it to still another person, my late
brother, Vladimir, to finish. In this way we formed a triumvirate. After everything had been written, we didn't know what pseudonym to sign to our common
play. Working for us was a valet, Kuz'ma Frolov, a fine old man whom we
loved well. Brother Vladimir and I said to him, "You know, Kuz'ma, we have
written a little book, and why don't you give us your name for it as if you had
written it.[1]

But Kuz'ma asked if the book was clever or not, and when they answered
that it was not, he refused to sign his name to it, so that ultimately the

---

[1] Koz'ma Prutkov, ed. P. N. Berkov, pp. 514-17.

triumvirate decided on the name Koz'ma Prutkov, instead of Kuz'ma Frolov.[2] Later, the worthy valet was called "Prutkov" instead of his real name by some people who had heard the rumor, widespread before this article, that Koz'ma Prutkov's name came from Žemčužnikov's valet.[3] Aleksej Žemčužnikov later claimed in a letter to the editor of *Novoe vremja (New Times)* that the article contained inaccuracies.[4] This statement has not been explored by critics, since there are no other clues to go on in what the brothers said or wrote.

The actual manner in which Prutkov was named sounds typical of the cousins. They did indeed have a valet named Kuz'ma Frolov. The name Kuz'ma sounds more Russian than Koz'ma, which is closer to the Greek Kosmâs and thus more high-flown. But why they chose the name *Prutkov* is not fully explained by them or by subsequent critics. *Prut* in Russian means a switch (made from a single twig) and suggests the same whiplashing quality as the name Xlestakov. But there is an additional probable source for the name in France. Most likely the name Prutkov, which became a byword in Russia, was taken from an equally famous fictitious French personage: Joseph Prudhomme, whom Henri Bonaventure Monnier (1805–1877) had created a few years earlier.[5] The name Joseph Prudhomme and Koz'ma Prutkov have a similar sound, and the characters also resemble one another. Monnier invented a caricature of the Parisian bourgeois of the 1830's who is to this day as well-known to the French-speaking world as Koz'ma Prutkov is to the Russian. (The French name suggests bourgeois prudence.) The resemblance goes deeper than the sound of the name. Monnier was also a *mystificateur* who played practical jokes.[6] He was even better known as an artist and made his début in 1830 with his *Scènes populaires dessinées*

[2]   The first name was used with several variants in different works as they were first published. Thus, the name "Kuz'ma" was used in all the journal publications, "Koz'ma" in a portrait signature of 1853, and "Kos'ma" in the alphabet of 1861. The name Koz'ma was finally canonized in 1876 when "Some Materials for the biography of K. P. Prutkov" appeared in the *Sankt-Peterburgskie vedomosti*, No. 110 (April 22, 1876).
[3]   S. Luk'janov, *O Vl. Solov'eve v ego molodye gody* (Petersburg, 1921), III, 237-38.
[4]   See P. N. Berkov, *Koz'ma Prutkov, direktor probirnoj palatki i poet*, p. 13.
[5]   The only French critic of Prutkov calls him "un type de Prudhomme russe", but does not press the point further—not even to mention the similar sound of the names. See André Lirondelle, *Le poète Alexis Tolstoi, l'homme et l'oeuvre*, p. 78. D. S. Mirsky also uses this very phrase in *A History of Russian Literature* (New York: Vintage Books, 1958), p. 234. See also A. A. Morozov, *Russkaja stixotvornaja parodija (XVII-načalo XXv.)* (Leningrad, 1960), p. 61.
[6]   Champfleury, *Henry Monnier, sa vie, son oeuvre* (Paris: E. Dentu, 1879), pp. 144-57.

à la plume, including a portrait and signature facsimile of Joseph Prudhomme (as we shall see, Prutkov's portrait also became famous). Monnier too wrote vaudevilles, the most famous of which was the *Grandeur
et décadence de M. Joseph Prudhomme*, in which he himself played the
lead. It was first shown in Paris in 1852, exactly the same year Prutkov
was named. (Perhaps Tolstoj or one of the Žemčužnikovs followed the
Parisian theatrical season in reviews.) Prudhomme became famous in
France and many other writers pirated his name in their works (the same
fate befell Prutkov).

In his most famous work, the *Mémoires*, Prudhomme interposes trivial
anecdotes with fatuous thoughts of his own, such as the "réflexions pro-
fondes et justes sur l'incertitude des décisions humaines".[7] In the beginning he says people have compelled him to write his memoirs ("mes con-
temporains l'ont voulu"). He says further, "je prétends, selon l'usage
universellement adopté aujourd'hui, me dresser de mon vivant un pédest-
al sur lequel les siècles futurs pourront me contempler tout à leur aise."[8]
Prudhomme's egotism is as boundless as Prutkov's, but Monnier's satiric
critique of society is more heavily pronounced. All of France is bourgeois, says Prudhomme; Prutkov would never go so far as to say that
the bureaucracy is taking over Russia. Finally, Prudhomme's *mots*, his
incredible metaphors, are quite like those of Prutkov. For instance,
claiming aristocratic birth, he says: "L'auteur de mes jours aurait pu
porter sa tête sur l'échafaud, comme tant d'autres, s'il n'était mort d'un
catarrhe pulmonaire dans la fleur de sa vieillesse."[9] Granted their great
national differences, Prutkov and Prudhomme are brothers under the
skin, and it is highly probable that Prutkov's cultivated tutors thought
of this well-known French creation when they named their Russian one.

The chronology in Žemčužnikov's article is also unclear. Some time
had elapsed between the writing of *Fantasia* and the naming of Prutkov,
but Aleksej does not say how much. During that time *Fantasia* had been
performed (the authors calling themselves "Y" and "Z") and several
humorous fables had been published. In a letter to A. N. Pypin on
February 6, 1883, Vladimir Žemčužnikov filled in some of the missing
facts about Prutkov:

> ...The image... of Koz'ma Prutkov, as my brother has said, was created
> not all of a sudden but gradually, autonomously as it were, and only later was

---

[7]   Henri Monnier, *Mémoires de monsieur Joseph Prudhomme* (Paris: Librairie nouvelle, 1857), p. 21.
[8]   *Ibid.*, p. 2.
[9]   *Ibid.*

filled out and completed consciously by us. Some things which have been
included in the works of Koz'ma Prutkov were written even earlier than the
representation in our minds of a single creator. ... At first we simply wrote
out of merriment, without any concern to invest what was written with any
common characteristic at all besides merriment and mockery. Nevertheless
this did not continue. ... In 1850 we wrote the vaudeville-joke *Fantasia*,
signed Y and Z, given in December of that year at the Aleksandrinskij theater... and immediately banned by command of highest authority (i.e., the
Emperor). ... Then in the summer of 1851 or 1852[10] when our family (without
Count Tolstoj) was staying ... in the country, my brother Aleksandr composed,
completely as a joke, the fable "Forget-me-nots and Footboards"; this form
of poetic prank was to our taste and (we) wrote (more) fables. ... At that
time the figure of Koz'ma Prutkov was not yet born. However, these fables
made us think ... and upon our return to St. Petersburg, gave me, my brother
Aleksej and Count A. Tolstoj (my brother Aleksandr was in service in Orenburg
at the time) the idea of writing as one personage, capable of all kinds of works.
This thought appealed to us, and we created the character of Koz'ma Prutkov.
By the summer of 1853, when we were back in the country, ... quite a few
of these works were collected and the comedy *Lace* was added ... In the fall,
with the agreement of A. Tolstoj and my brother Aleksej, I finally began the
final editing of everything we had prepared and gave it ... to Iv. Iv. Panaev for
print in *The Contemporary*.[11]

Thus Koz'ma Prutkov must have been born in 1852. Vladimir confirms
this in the "Biographical Information about Koz'ma Prutkov" which
he also wrote in 1883 especially for the *Complete Works:* "In that year
(1852) there occurred a deep change in his personality under the influence
of three persons ... (who) took him under their tutelage and developed
in him those typical qualities which made him known under the name of
Koz'ma Prutkov. He became confident, self-satisfied, trenchant."[12] This
was Prutkov's real birth. His fictional birth on April 11, 1803, and the
fictional life which ensued, will be discussed later, for they are part of
the art of fictional biography.

Prutkov's real career, in the journals of the day, began in earnest in
February 1854, when he first published in his own name in *The Contemporary*. Roughly half the works of Prutkov appeared in this journal.
It was natural for his creators to direct his work there, since they were
well acquainted with the literary circle of *The Contemporary*. Aleksej
Žemčužnikov had printed his comedy *Strannaja noč'* (*A Strange Night*)
there in 1850, and the brothers their three fables in 1851. *The Contem-*

---

[10]   It must have been in 1851, for three fables were first published anonymously in the
November, 1851 issue of *Sovremennik*.
[11]   Koz'ma Prutkov, pp. 395-96.
[12]   *Ibid.*, pp. 331-41.

porary was already known for its light verse and parody. The verses of the New Poet (Panaev's pseudonym) had appeared in Belinskij's lifetime, in the journal's first issue in 1847. In the section "Smes'"("Miscellanea"), light verse and parody continued. When the editors, Nekrasov and Panaev, received Prutkov's "Dosugi" ("Leisure Musings"), they decided to create a special section of the journal called "Literary Hodgepodge" ("Literaturnij eralaš"), a section entirely devoted to parody and humor. Works by Koz'ma Prutkov—aphoristic, poetic, and dramatic—occupied a major place in five of the issues in 1854. Five and a half years after this outburst had ceased, seven poems by Prutkov appeared in *The Contemporary* under the bilingual heading "Pux i per'ja (Daunen und Federn)",[13] but manuscript datings attest that most of these poems had been written in 1855 or earlier.

At that time *The Contemporary* had a new satirical section called "Svistok" ("The Whistle"). Prutkov's verses were printed first in its fourth number (March, 1860) and subsequently in four of the other five issues of "Svistok". Launched in 1859 with a preface by Dobroljubov, "Svistok" contained more satire than parody, more prose than poetry. It is to these years of *The Contemporary* that the critic A. A. Morozov refers when he states that "the outwardly harmless humorous parody of Prutkov, assumed in the context of *The Contemporary* a satirical orientation and supported the journal's struggle against the aestheticism of the forties and fifties."[14] Prutkov's creators did not view their verse in the same light as did Dobroljubov, who regarded it as a slap in the face of aestheticism and found parody in general "useful" so long as such poetry was being written, but declared that "the kind of parody directed exclusively against artistic insufficiencies of former poets was doomed to oblivion", because "pure art" had already been defeated.[15] (Dobroljubov characteristically equated artistic insufficiencies with a dearth of doctrine.) Some later critics persist in claiming that Prutkov specifically parodies "pure art",[16] the label which radicals pasted on poetry, whether excellent or bad, that claimed to be nothing more than poetry. In fact, Prutkov's creators engaged in no polemics with any one school of writing. They parodied whatever struck them as ridiculous, literary phenomena both

---

[13] The name was taken from a sign over a German warehouse on the Vassil'ev island. See "Polnoe sobranie sočinenija K. Prutkova", *Vestnik Evropy*, No. 3 (1884), p. 393.
[14] A. A. Morozov, *Russkaja stixotvornaja parodija (XVII-načalo XX v.)*, p. 60.
[15] N. A. Dobroljubov, "Sovremennoe obozrenie", *Sovremennik*, No. 8 (1860), 290.
[16] See, for one of numerous Soviet arguments, V. Desnickij in Koz'ma Prutkov, *Izbrannye sočinenija* (Leningrad: 1953), pp. 5-29.

persistent (such as lyricism without even poetic logic) and short-lived (such as the neo-classical vogue).

Prutkov did not write for these satiric journals; he just happened to publish in them. Thus, more Prutkovian aphorisms and anecdotes (called by Vladimir "primarily the weakest"[17]) were published in four numbers of the satiric journal *The Spark* in 1860. The last contribution to *The Contemporary* came in 1863 when, after Dobroljubov's death, Saltykov-Ščedrin published in the ninth and last issue of "Svistok" the "Necrology of Koz'ma Prutkov" and his "Posthumous Works", including the truly satirical "Proekt: O vvedenii edinomyslija v Rossii" ("A Projekt for the Introduction of Unity of Thought in Russia") which preceded Saltykov's own similar projects in "Dnevnik provinciala v Peterburge" and "Pestrye pis'ma".

After 1863, hardly a word was heard from the real Koz'ma Prutkov for twenty years, but during that time his name was often taken in vain by other parodists who never came close to sounding truly Prutkovian. The best of these minor Prutkovs was, as we have seen, Aleksandr Žemčužnikov with his 1876 publications. Some imitators used other names. As early as 1864, *The Spark* printed I. Maslov's anecdotes, similar to those of Prutkov. In the same journal appeared vaguely Prutkovian epigrams written by everybody on the staff. Others imitated even more blatantly: in 1876 D. D. Minaev, the translator and parodist, published works "from the notebooks of K. Prutkov Jr."; aphorisms signed Prutkov appeared in *Budil'nik (The Alarm Clock)*; more such aphorisms were printed in No. 49 of *The Petersburg Gazette* in 1876; and, most notably, the writer M. A. Filippov published a whole series of works in the journal *Vek (Century)* in 1882–83 and signed them "Prutkov, the 2nd, Kuz'ma", and even "K. Prutkov". Filippov apparently thought, as did many others, that Koz'ma Prutkov was a pseudonym thought up by the journal *The Contemporary*, used by Nekrasov, Panaev, and Dobroljubov as well as others, and thus was nobody's private property. Vladimir and Aleksej Žemčužnikov heatedly protested such behavior,[18] but no letters or repeated protests had as much success in defending the memory of the real Prutkov as did the *Complete Works* which finally appeared in 1884. After that date, as we have seen, Prutkov was often mentioned in books and journals, but these writings had the tone of fond remembrances, coming well after the death of his creators.

---

[17]   Koz'ma Prutkov, p. 331.
[18]   *Ibid.*, pp. 386-92.

They did not attempt to plagiarize Prutkov's style or to capitalize on his name.

Part of the problem stemmed from the fact that Prutkov was a literary *mistifikacija*. In keeping with the pretense that Prutkov's works were the creation of a single author, the number of participants as well as their identity was kept secret for a long time, so that, as we have seen, Prutkov remained a mystery even in literary circles. It was rumored at various times that Panaev, Nekrasov, Dobroljubov, Ammosov (who did write one fable included in Prutkov's canonized works), the literary historian Longinov and others in *The Contemporary* circle took part in Prutkovian writings. Occasionally they were ascribed to only one of the brothers, as in 1873 in N. V. Gerbel's "Russkie pisateli v biografijax i obrazax", which provoked Aleksej's denial that Prutkov was his alone[19]—the first revelation of Prutkov's true identity by one of the real authors. In the "Biographical Facts" which serve as an introduction to the *Complete Works*, Vladimir begins in a tone of joking *mistifikacija* but ends by naming not only Aleksej Tolstoj, his brothers Aleksej and Aleksandr and himself, but also their friend P. P. Eršov (known in Russian literature as the author of the verse fairy-tale "Konek-Gorbunok", "The Little Hunch-backed Horse") whose role, as we shall see, was decidedly minor. Thus what had begun informally as a mystifying joke became a book by an author whose real identity was known to all, but whose fictitious biography, taken as such, appeared more interesting than any reality.

The publication of the *Complete Works* ended forever the career of the real Koz'ma Prutkov in Russian journals, although some lost works were rediscovered and published in Soviet ones. P. N. Berkov, the pioneer in Prutkov scholarship, made the important point that "contrary to wide spread belief, the *Complete Works* of Koz'ma Prutkov were not a result of the previous printing of separate poems, but on the contrary, the journalistic publications were printed as a result of the impossibility of realizing the projected edition of the *Complete Works*."[20] Thus, the journals served as an outlet for writings that would not appear as a whole book, but the reason is still unclear.

In the "Biographical Facts" we are told that "in the first year of (Prutkov's) public literary activity (in 1853), he already occupied himself

---

[19]   *Ibid.*, pp. 379-80.
[20]   P. N. Berkov, "Neizdannye i zabytye proizvedenija Koz'my Prutkova", *Literaturnoe nasledstvo*, III (1932), 217.

with the preparation of a separate edition of his works with a portrait."[21] The existence of the portrait (more than their Prutkovian statements) proves the intentions of the brothers. It was sketched and lithographed in 1853 by another Žemčužnikov brother, Lev, and by two of his fellow art students, A. E. Bejdeman and L. F. Lagorio. The censor, afraid it might be a caricature of an official person, banned the lithograph and Vladimir Žemčužnikov tells us merely that "consequently the whole edition was not printed".[22] In any case, it became clear somehow in 1853 (whether because of censorship, unofficial warning, cautiousness, or stubbornness) that the complete works would not be published in book form, and then later that year many of them were given to *The Contemporary*.

Many nonsense writers have illustrated their own work, or have inspired others to illustrate them.[23] The simplest line of written humor seems to suggest an abundance of pictorial images. Prutkov's face later became as famous as his words, and it forms the frontispiece for most editions of his work. He is magnificently ugly, with unkempt hair, shaggy brows, a snub nose, coarse half-parted lips, a dimple in his chin, and a couple of large warts. His whole face bears an expression of proud disdain and his ringed hand is clenched to his puffed-out chest in a gesture of romantic defiance.

Letters and archival documents bear witness that Vladimir Žemčužnikov still worked on the *Complete Works* after this setback—in 1859, 1865, and 1876.[24] The actual publication was done by M. M. Stasjulevič, editor of *Vestnik Evropy* (the *European Messenger*), to which Aleksej Žemčužnikov was a frequent contributor. Vladimir prepared the edition and Aleksej looked over all the manuscripts. The importance of the *Complete Works* in establishing the final image of Koz'ma Prutkov cannot be overestimated, although critics have neglected this. Vladimir's arrangements of the book's contents, preceding each section with a sort of Prutkovian preamble, gave the works a unity which overpowered their generic and genetic variety. It diminished the importance of the fact

---

[21] Koz'ma Prutkov, p. 339.

[22] *Ibid.* Some people have noticed a similarity between the portrait of Koz'ma Prutkov and the head of Peter I on the statue of the "bronze horseman". Those holding this view would have the support of A. S. Orlov, Ju. N. Tynjanov and the present writer. On the other hand, P. N. Berkov believes that it is a composite of separate features of Prutkov's creators: Koz'ma Prutkov, ed. P. N. Berkov, p. 597.

[23] For examples: Edward Lear's *Book of Nonsense* and *Nonsense Songs*, most of Lewis Carroll's works, Kipling's *Just So Stories*, G. K. Chesterton's *Biography for Beginners* and *Greybeards at Play*, or the works of Alfred Jarry.

[24] Koz'ma Prutkov, p. 25, Buxštab has found a censor's license for the "Dosugi" dated December 30, 1859. *Ibid.*, p. 423.

that any single work was a parody of any particular author. It permanently transformed the works of Aleksej Tolstoj and the brothers Žemčužnikov into the works of Koz'ma Prutkov. Nearly every previous work was republished, with slight and usually improving changes. As we shall see, these usually involved the changing of a word to increase absurdity and the pruning out of weaker quatrains. The highly satirical "Project" was omitted, apparently at the last moment, for its prepared text exists among Aleksej Žemčužnikov's papers. Either he or some outside source must have cautioned Vladimir against printing it. The military aphorisms were also excluded, probably for the same reason. Few new poems were added. As we have seen, most of Aleksandr's works were excluded. Most important, Vladimir added subtitles to many poems previously published without them, and these point to the parodied author—Benediktov, Fet, Polonskij, Xomjakov, Grigoriev, I. Aksakov or Ščerbina. In 1884 it might have been difficult to determine without such subtitles the specific writers Prutkov parodied or indeed whether the works were parodies at all. Vladimir Žemčužnikov apparently felt that if these poems were perceived as parody, another dimension would be added to the reader's appreciation. Although scholars sometimes go too far in trying to discover work by a certain author which most exactly resembles the one written by Prutkov, further elucidations of the origins of Prutkovian verse have added to the modern reader's appreciation. Thus, the changes wrought by Vladimir Žemčužnikov in canonizing the works of Prutkov were mostly additive. But because of these additions, especially the prose footnotes and the biographical data, and because for the first time the reader hears at one stretch his insistent voice, Koz'ma Prutkov himsele sets the tone of his works.

Koz'ma Prutkov is not entirely without antecedents in Russian literature. To say, as has one critic, that "Koz'ma Prutkov is a *unicum;* he has neither predecessors nor followers"[25] is only partial truth. Prutkov's original home can be found not only in family wit and pranks, but also in the salons and the feuilletons of the forties and earlier. Poets like S. A. Neelov (1779–1852), I. P. Mjatlev (1796–1844) and S. A. Sobolevskij (1803–1870) wrote epigrams, fables, or lyrics, and shone in impromptu renderings and creations of their verse. Many, indeed perhaps the flower, of their verses have been lost or preserved only second-hand in the

---

[25] N. A. Kotljarevskij, "Starinnye portrety. Graf Aleksej Tolstoj kak satirik", *Vestnik Evropy*, IV (July, 1906), 47.

memoirs of their contemporaries.[26] They spoke and wrote it in their own names, and without Prutkovian sententiousness. Their epigrams, unlike Prutkov's, were usually directed against someone, in the traditional style. Their light verse usually ended with a true, not an illogical, *pointe*. Mjatlev, whom Lermontov admired in his late (1841) poem "In the Album of S. N. Karamzina", and in whose style Lermontov occasionally wrote, used to read his verses as if he were having a conversation.[27] He resembles Prutkov the most. For instance, in his poem "Raút",[28] the short lines tumble out with clever rhyme, foreign words, and Prutkovian insouciance. It ends a description of an evening ruined by card-playing with the lines:

А в раýт	And to cards
Все бегут,	Everyone runs
Как в беседу.	As to a debate.
Нет, нет, нет!	No, no, no!
Се тро бет,	C'est trop bête:
Не поеду!	I won't go!

Like Prutkov, the poem has rapid, innocent humor and the card-terms and foreign words bring it closer to nonsense-poetry.

A later and quite different literary trend also resembles Prutkov. In the late forties and early fifties a new phenomenon appeared in some Russian journals. From about 1847, *The Contemporary*, under Nekrasov's new editorship, published many fewer verses and many more verse parodies. These parodies were composed by writers of feuilletons who tended to assume fixed pseudonyms, usually negative or grotesque. Thus separate parodies congealed into one image or, as one critic described this trend, parody turned into parodic cycles, "the cyclicization of separate parodic attempts".[29] Much of this parody still carried the personal, intimate tone of the salon, and indeed many journals seemed to be private clubs, existing for their members' entertainment. The outsiders were

---

[26]   Nevertheless, some of their works have been published. See, for Neelov: *Russkie propilei*, II (Moscow, 1916); for Mjatlev: *Polnoe sobranie sočinenij I. P. Mjatleva* (St. Petersburg, 1857); for Sobolevskij: *Epigrammy i eksprompty S. A. Sobolevskogo*, ed. V. V. Kallaš (Moscow, 1912).
[27]   See *Poety 1840-1850-x godov*, ed. B. Ja. Buxštab and V. S. Kiseleva (Moscow–Leningrad, 1962), p. 90.
[28]   *Ibid.*, pp. 117-19.
[29]   J. G. Oksman, ed., *Fel'etony sorokovyx godov* (Moscow–Leningrad: Academia, 1930), pp. 352-59.

supposed to guess the real author of the feuilleton and this guessing game was part of the joke. Often the name represented a collective effort; hence the misconception that Koz'ma Prutkov was the creation of the entire staff of *The Contemporary*.

But the literary mask Prutkov most closely resembles was worn by a single man, I. I. Panaev. Under the name of the "New Poet", Panaev parodied the same victims that Prutkov would later pick: Benediktov, Xomjakov, Ščerbina, Polonskij, Fet, and the would-be Heines. His versatility in style-imitation was remarkable, but Panaev did not always seize upon the particular foible of his victim and render it sufficiently grotesque, so that his poems often seem to be what Prutkov claimed his were—not parody, but imitation.

Thus, while no one poet or trend duplicates Prutkov, he often seems to have the finesse of the salon or the parodic devices of the feuilletons; and without such a poetic and parodic atmosphere, it is doubtful that Koz'ma Prutkov would have drawn breath.

Prutkov's followers are less numerous than his predecessors, and their works belong to a different chapter of the history of Russian literature. They are not the obvious imitators who filled the journals of the sixties and seventies; these epigoni took aim from a position too close to their target, turning parody into satire. None of their created parodic personae have at the same time the defined personality of Prutkov and the range of his poetic "experience". D. D. Minaev's retired Major Burbonov is a parodic image of Fet and, unlike Prutkov, depends on this parody for his own personality. Dobroljubov's Konrad Liliensvager is a hodgepodge of ideas and styles, often parodying more than one author or work at a time. Dobroljubov saw a similarity in social outlook among several people he parodied, but he fails to make his parody as clear as his views. Burbonov and Liliensvager are nearly forgotten today as names; Prutkov as a parodic literary figure remains without heirs.

The true heritage of Prutkov can be found in the lighter moments of highly serious writers, Dostoevskij and Vladimir Solov'ev. We shall see in Chapter V how Dostoevskij used a poem by Prutkov in *The Village of Stepanchikovo*, incorporating its humor into his own comic novel. Solov'ev wrote parodies of Prutkovian excellence on the Symbolists and on himself. In his Prutkovian mystery-comedy, *Belaja lilija (The White Lily)*, he wrote:

Таков закон: все лучшее в тумане,
А близкое иль больно, иль смешно.

Such is the law: the best things are in fog,
What's close is either painful or comic.

These self-mocking lines also contain a clue to the reason for his humor. Like Prutkov's guardians, Solov'ev was able at times to turn a threatening vision into something comic.[30]

---

[30] Prutkov's later successors in the late 1920's were the Oberjuty with their black, surrealist humor. See George Gibian, trans. and ed., *Russia's Lost Literature of the Absurd* (Ithaca: Cornell University Press, 1971).

III

THE PLAYS:
COMIC VARIETY AND PRUTKOVIAN TRADEMARKS

Prutkov's interest lies not just in his strange literary genesis and his peculiar relationship to the biographies of his creators. Speaking strictly of his works, what sets Prutkov apart from either his predecessors or his followers is the delicate balance in his writing between two kinds of voices: the peculiar Prutkovian voice crowing over its creation, speaking loudly and condescendingly to the reader, and the more gentlemanly voice of his "guardians", in the whimsical turn taken by the work itself. Prutkov's voice is heard most loudly in his prose, for his narrative and didactic manners are naturally the most self-imposing. In the introductions, footnotes, aphorisms and biographies he fairly shouts into the reader's ear. In the shorter verse, the balance between Prutkov's own voice and the tricks, parodic and poetic, of the poetry itself is maintained more completely than anywhere else. This balance and the brevity of most of the poems give them both lightness and intricacy.

But in his plays Prutkov is scarcely heard and then only in the stage directions, a normal enough phenomenon when one considers that the playwright is more remote from his audience than the lyric poet or the essayist, since he speaks exclusively through the actors. The dramatis persona may be as close or closer to the reader-spectator than the lyric persona, but he stands further from the author. Prutkov is a pseudo-author, however, and the pseudo-plays he wrote, when taken together, have something distinctly Prutkovian; no plays quite like them have been written before or since. Subtitled vaudeville, proverb, scene in verse, operetta, conversation, mystery and drama, their ostensible variety masks their Prutkovian unity, and this is part of the joke. No matter in what genre he wrote, it was always Prutkov writing.

The plays of Prutkov belong to that sub-class or cousin of parody known as burlesque. They imitate not a specific author or work but a style or a genre. Their humor is often coarse, but even when subtle, it intends to entertain, not to criticize or correct.

Fantasia, perhaps the first Tolstoj-Žemčužnikov collaboration, has an unusual fate to match its highly unusual method of composition. The performance of *Fantasia* marked the cousins' decision to take their literary pranks into the larger world of St. Petersburg, where not just friends and family but also complete strangers could hear them. These strangers proved, in addition, to be strangers to the humor of the play. On the evening of January 8, 1851, *Fantasia* was first (and last) performed at the Aleksandrinskij Theater; it puzzled and therefore offended not only critics[1] and minor officials, but also the most critical and major official of them all, the Tsar himself. Nicholas I had consecrated his twenty-five-year reign to the maintenance of order and decorum. *Fantasia* is one long breach of decorum. Its characters undercut each other and behave grotesquely, alternating flattery and insult without apparent motivation.

Nicholas had probably expected to see just another amusing vaudeville, in which characters behaved conventionally and all ended well. The four other plays on the bill with *Fantasia* were comedies of just that sort. Their titles tell much about them; they were called *Ardor Began to Speak, or a Lesson for a Devilish Girl*; *The Attractive Widower, or the Nocturnal Rendezvous with Illuminations*; *The Fellow from the Provinces*; and *Actors' Evening*.[2] *Fantasia* followed these vaudevilles on the program, but turned their customary techniques into burlesque. One of the most high-spirited works of its time, *Fantasia* also contains elements of farce, with its underlying violence which produces a reaction of shock in the audience.

Written for a joke, as we have seen, *Fantasia* was originally called a "šutka-vodevil'".[3] The Russian vaudeville comedy, which had its first period of development in the 1810's and 1820's, became most popular

---

[1]   That the critics disliked *Fantasia* is evident from the following reviews: F. Koni, "Teatral'naja letopis", *Panteon*, I (1851), 12-13; M. D. *Otečestvennye zapiski*, LXXIV (February, 1851), 227; P. M. Zotov, "Teatral'naja xronika", *Severnaja pčela*, No. 13 (January 19, 1851), p. 3. Fedor Koni, a veteran vaudeville writer himself, missed the joke; however, a more sensitive critic of literary trends, Apollon Grigor'ev, who had not seen the play but had read Koni's review, understood that *Fantasia* reduced to absurdity certain elements in contemporary plays. He wrote: "The parody of Messrs. Y and Z could not be a success because the hour of the fall of the works parodied by them has not yet come." *Moskvitjanin*, No. 6 (1851), p. 278.

[2]   In the original: "*Zagovorilo retivoe, ili urok besovoj devuške*; *Interesnyj vdovec, ili Nočnoe svidanie s illjuminaciej*; *Provincial'nyj bratec*; and *Večer artistov*.

[3]   CGALI, Fond 639, opis' 2, ed. xr. 17.

in the 1830's and early 1840's, when Russia was suffering from a real dearth of good repertory plays. *Fantasia* was written in 1850 when vaudeville was coming to a natural end, being replaced by a more serious comedy of manners, a comedy of characters rather than of intrigue, with a specifically Russian rather than a generalized setting, showing contemporary Russian mores in a satiric light. Later writers like Suxovo-Kobylin would make extensive use of vaudeville in their plays, but as a pure genre it was dead by the end of the 1850's. *Fantasia* helped dig its grave while it was only moribund.

Vaudeville's most characteristic features are a blending of dramatic action with musical couplets (which in good vaudeville are motivated by the text) and a concluding moral. As a genre it is close to situation comedy and to comic opera. Like situation comedy, its content—invariably a love intrigue—is not profound, and the ending is bound to be happy. Freed from concern for the characters, the spectator can focus his full attention upon the intricacy of the unfolding plot. But the text is more important than in comic opera; it is not merely an excuse for breaking into song. Rather, the song breaks into it.

The two cousins used all these conventions, but did so over-enthusiastically, thereby turning them to parody. They also added certain highly improper elements to an already exaggerated genre. For example, vaudevilles generally had large numbers of actors in them; the cousins added to them still more actors "without lines", namely dogs of all sorts. If characters in vaudeville are distinguished only by superficial traits, why shouldn't dogs of various breeds claim proper roles as well?

The typical vaudeville plot revolves around a pair of lovers who overcome all obstacles in a happy ending. *Fantasia*, like Gogol's *Ženit'ba*, multiplies the young hero into a whole flock of suitors, and centers the action around choosing a husband for Lizaveta Platonovna, the ward of Čupurlina, "a rich but vain old lady". (Note the Prutkovian uncontradictory contradiction.) The six suitors who present themselves have fantastic, evocative surnames, descriptions which often contradict these names, and behavior which contradicts either or both. For instance, Batog-Batyev is not a ferocious Tartar but a soap-merchant, and Kutilo-Zavaldajskij is not a carouser but a "respectable man" whose whole life is spent living down his name and who persecutes others with spectres of correctness. Bespardonnyj, far from impudent, is a "shy man". One character has a typical eighteenth-century "positive" name, Milovidov, although he is slovenly in appearance and blatantly interested only in the size of the dowry. Throughout, human relationships are dehumanized. The old lady is more interested in her dog than her ward, but Lizaveta seems not to care. Perhaps this is a parody on the misunderstood ward, like Puškin's Lizaveta Ivanovna in *Pikovaja dama* who is treated ironically at the end of the story, when she marries and has a ward of her own. The action takes place at Čupurlina's country-house, a typical Russian comic-opera setting, with the usual props: a summer-house and a fountain. Only the summer-house is "very narrow" and sports a flag bearing the inscription "What is our life?" and the fountain is "very small". As the curtain opens, the various suitors pace back and forth amid these shrunken objects in a "prolonged silence". Finally there is a heated debate about the time. The clock strikes seven, but one of the suitors has only two-thirty. Libental' sets himself apart by remarking that he hasn't brought a watch, "for (aside) the happy do not notice the hours". The whole dialogue has no dramatic motivation; it exists merely to introduce Libental's pun (časy means both watch and hours), a famous line from Griboedov's *Woe from Wit*. This opening scene is typical of the movement of the whole play.

The suitors then state the purpose of their visit and the main question of the play: "Who will receive the hand of Lizaveta Platonovna? That is the question!" leaving no doubt in the audience's mind and leaving the suitors free to compose for their hostess a "pleasant compliment in the form of a fine couplet and sing, as the actors and actresses usually do on-stage in any vaudeville." After certain poetic blunders and some false starts, they write new words to "Frère Jacques":

Вот куплеты	Here are some couplets,
Мы поэты	We poets,
В вашу честь (*bis*)	In your honor! (repeat)
Написали вместе,	Wrote them together,
На своем всяк месте.	Each in his own place.
Здесь нас шесть!	There are six of us here!
Нас здесь шесть!	Six of us there are here!

Besides being something of a tongue-twister, this ditty also describes the way *Fantasia* was written: "(we) wrote together, each in his own place." The old lady enters, thanks them, and asks them all how rich they are, all the while caressing her pug-dog. Batog-Batyev hands out samples of soap; the others are less definite, but the clever German Libental' admires the dog. The old lady decides to give her ward to him, in spite of a whispered denunciation by one of the other suitors. Libental' "hops silently for a while on one leg" and then proposes to the young lady, who is as silent and wooden a heroine as one might find in any vaudeville. The young pair burst into song, but are interrupted several times by various servants searching for Fantazija, the pug-dog. They gaze into each other's eyes while the stage becomes crowded with frantic searchers. The old lady now says she will give Lizaveta to the one who brings her Fantazija back. The suitors are back where they started, and in no less than twenty asides to the audience they plot their separate schemes to retrieve the dog or find a new one, and the act ends in song, this time to a tune probably from *La Cenerentola* (the authors give only its first line).

A "little interlude" follows, during which (possibly for the first and last time in the theater) only dogs appear onstage. As a storm breaks, the pug-dog runs across the stage followed by an "unknown bulldog", while the orchestra plays a tune from *The Barber of Seville*. This little intermission was inserted, we recall, in order to glue together the two acts of the play, written by the two cousins. At this point, adding to the spectacle, the Tsar "arose from his seat with a look of dissatisfaction on his face and left the theater".[4]

The suitors return in the next scene and sing about how they have not found the dog. "We are all without Fantasy", one of them exclaims, quite aptly. Libental', however, has not yet made his appearance, and they all fear that he will have the necessary Fantasy. One suitor proposes another dog called "Kosmopolit", and the old lady asks, "Čem palit?" The other suitors offer other dogs, all of which occasion puns, some of which indicate that the dogs were not housebroken (the censor eliminated all these shocking references). The old lady decides to give her ward to the suitor with another pug-dog similar to Fantasija, but Lizaveta Plato-novna objects strenuously. Evidently she has fallen in love with Libental'. The old lady gives them her blessing anyway, and at this heart-rending moment Libental' runs onstage with the real Fantasija, as the ladies faint. He naturally gets the heroine, and the disgruntled suitors sing an-other song to the tune of "Frère Jacques", only this time with uncompli-mentary words. The plot has been nicely resolved and ended in song, but where is the moral?

When everyone else has left the stage, Kutilo-Zavaldajskij steps to the footlights and turns to the orchestra. He asks the double-bass for the program, is given it, and says, "I am very curious to see who is the

---

[4] The authors of *Fantasia* were absent that evening (they were attending a ball), but eyewitnesses to the event included Tolstoj's mother and Žemčužnikov's father and brothers. One of them, Lev, related this story to Aleksej who recorded it many years later. See Koz'ma Prutkov, pp. 401-402.

author of this play." Of course no name did appear on the program, and he wonders aloud how the management could permit such a play. He claims that the prompter kept whispering the most improper lines to him, but he refused to speak them and made up other ones. He objects to the plot and outlines several other ones which he would substitute, but the curtain falls behind him, the orchestra interrupts him, and he runs off. Many members of the audience thought that the actor Martynov improvised this speech, and applauded him loudly.

The moral is that when one plot is as good as another, why not give free reign to all else—puns, asides, amorous improbabilities, dogs, the actor's own ideas, and above all, the fantasy of the authors. The play has been made as artificial and as self-mocking as possible, more vaude-villian than vaudeville itself. The obsession of various characters with propriety (the word "prilično" appears repeatedly), their own and that of the author, is of cardinal importance. The feigned fear of not conforming to propriety or to theatrical convention, when voiced, engenders the breaking of all convention, and this is precisely what the cousins had in mind. The play, embellished by boos and hisses from the audience, the Tsar's departure, bad reviews and an official ban, caused a scandal like few others in the history of the Russian theater.

Although not strictly a play by Koz'ma Prutkov, *Fantasia* had the opportunity of becoming one, quite unintentionally. A flesh-and-blood Koz'ma Prutkov, in the form of a censor named Gederstern (who, like Prutkov, held the rank of "dejstvitel'nyj statskij sovetnik") became extremely annoyed by the script and wrote all sorts of comments on a copy of it, making various trivial changes as well.[5] From these changes it becomes obvious that the censor knew a spirit of freethinking licentiousness floated somewhere through the play, but he could not locate it exactly. As a result, he struck aimlessly and often illogically at various words and phrases. He picked on a few coarse words (such as "glotka") and changed them to a more literary form ("gorlo"). For some unknown reason he crossed out the expression "Ax, ty besstydnik". He effaced all references to officials, even to a fireman. All references to religion, including the word "sacred" in "sacred duty", were omitted. Prudish as Prutkov, he crossed out a reference to a dog who "waters the flowers". Finally, he even presumed to help the authors by making stylistic changes, adding a noun to a lone adjective, or changing an adverb from "on purpose" to "quickly" for the sake of rhyme.

---

[5]   This script with corrections is preserved in the Puškinskij dom, Rukopis'nyj otdel.

When he put *Fantasia* into the *Complete Works of Koz'ma Prutkov*, Vladimir Žemčužnikov did just what was necessary to give the play the real Prutkovian stamp: he had Prutkov include all of the censor's remarks in footnotes, which were printed in the 1884 edition and in all editions thereafter. In all the history of Russian censorship, no one had thought of damning the censor in quite this way, by letting him be heard in the full tyranny of his pettiness. In this instance, his illogical grapplings with illogic itself could not have been more appropriate.

The other plays of Koz'ma Prutkov all parody contemporary theatrical trends by exaggerating their situations and devices. Almost every theatrical school provides a field for Prutkovian exercises—from the realistic, people-at-home plays (*Lace* and *The Rash Turk*) to the romantic-symbolic (*The Affinity of Universal Forces*). Only one play, *The Triumph of Virtue*, is a true satire, and it too involves the Prutkovian conflict between decorum and impropriety. In all eight of Koz'ma Prutkov's plays, written by Tolstoj and the Žemčužnikovs together and separately, the devil of impropriety wins the struggle.

Lace (*Blondy*), the first play composed under Prutkov's name, was written by Alexander Žemčužnikov with the aid of his brothers Aleksej and Vladimir in the summer of 1853. In it Prutkov answered some bad reviews received by a couple of Aleksej's comedies in *Moskvitjanin*. Žemčužnikov had been reproached by one reviewer[6] for not knowing enough about the high society he describes in his comedy *Sumasšedšij*. Prutkov answers by writing a high society play as the reviewer would have it, with grotesquely exaggerated situations and settings. Prutkov would be as remote from such a world, imply the Žemčužnikovs, as is the reviewer. Since another comedy by Aleksej, *Strannaja noc'*, had been compared in two reviews[7] to a Musset "proverbe", *Blondy* is called a "dramatic proverb in one act". With *Blondy* Prutkov silences Aleksej's critics (as he later silenced the censor of *Fantasia*) by following their suggestions to the letter and beyond.

The play has a small cast of characters, all suitably drawn from the highest social spheres: a Prince, a Princess, and a Baron. Instead of containing the triangular love plot which such a cast would seem to promise, the play involves a family squabble between the Prince and Princess. The Baron, an eavesdropping *raisonneur*, overhears their dispute and resolves it by pulling from his back pocket No. 22 of *Moskvitjanin*,

[6]   B. Almazov, *Moskvitjanin*, No. 22 (1852), pp. 37-42.
[7]   Koz'ma Prutkov, p. 449.

1852, and reading from a critic's statement on page thirty-nine that "the chief distinguishing feature of *bon ton* is courtesy *(učtivost')*". The Baron then admonishes the pair for not knowing what "even a journalist" understands. They agree and are happily reunited.

The play itself is funnier than the jibe, both because of the language of the aristocrats and the matter of their conversation. The trio speak a completely distorted, Gallicized Russian (hardly a new idea in Russian comedy), but as skillfully done as some of Fonvizin's best repartee. They use such expressions as: "peremenim materiju", "ty menja vyvodiš' iz terpenija", "ja trebuju ob'jasnenija vašix rezonov", "čto prinadležit do menja" (pour ma part), and "Ax! ne videl li menja kto-nibud' takim manerom?" There is also a pun in French, the ultimate in refinement ("Princess: 'Point de bêtise!' Baron: 'Point d'Alençon'.") Occasionally, however, the Prince slips into low Russian, as in "A ja počem znaju!"

Most of the conversation is about food, material furnishings and other adornments of high life. If the cast of characters is small, the list of objects present onstage is enormous. Prutkov has lavished many words on the setting; he is obviously full of vicarious enthusiasm for such luxury. Everything in the Princess' salon is "extraordinarily rich", "extraordinarily beautiful" and heavily gilded. Family portraits in heavy gilt frames hang on the rear wall. The "extraordinarily rich furniture" is scattered in "artistic disorder". The Princess enters with a cup of chocolate in one hand and an engraving in the other. The Prince spends most of his time eating or admiring the food, and the Princess reproachfully demands the lace he has promised but forgotten to buy her. The Baron buys the lace, gives the lesson in courtesy, and saves the day. As the curtain falls, the Prince promises his wife a new engraving, and we are sure the whole cycle will begin again. Such is Prutkov's depiction of an aristocratic slice-of-life.

Like *Lace*, *The Dispute of Ancient Greek Philosophers about the Elegant*, published in 1854, is about refined people who very nearly lose their polite restraint. Being Greek as well as philosophers, Klefiston and Stif (made-up "Greek" names) express only the noblest of emotions while they are disputing, but in rather unclassical fashion they preface each candidate for elegance with "I love" or "I like", thereby turning a philosophical search for excellence into a catalogue of personal preferences and a learned dispute into a fight.

The exact authorship of this play is unknown; more than one of the cousins loved to mock the nineteenth-century Russian imitators of ancient

Greece and in general "modern" people enjoy spoofing the "ancients".
The fact that the play may be a parody of Majkov, Fet, and especially
Ščerbina is unimportant; it stands by itself as a small theatrical and
poetic gem.

The scene is set somewhere in the environs of Athens and is "embellished with all the exquisite gifts of ancient Greek nature, that is: anem-
ones, serpents crawling around cisterns, blind-worms sucking pomegranates, acantha" (and the list continues, juxtaposing the beautiful with
the less beautiful). Sacrificial altars on gold tripods stand on either side
of the stage.

The two philosophers enter from opposite sides of backstage. Their
movements are of extreme importance throughout, for they walk "with
proud carriage and with plastic bodily motions" and extremely slowly —
just as Koz'ma Prutkov and any schoolboy would have Greeks move,
for he has seen them only as statues and his imagination is limited to that
representation. Both philosophers speak in variants of dactylic trimeter
with alternating rhymes. The humor stems as much from the exact
rhyming of foreign words with Russian ones as from the catalogue of
Greek habits.

К л е ф и с т о н : Часто лежу я под сенью дерев.
С т и ф :　　　Внемлю кузнечиков крикам.
К л е ф и с т о н : Нравится мне на стене барельеф.
С т и ф :　　　Я всё брожу под портиком!

Klefiston: I often lie under the canopy of trees.
Stif: I hark to the cries of grasshoppers.
Klefiston: I like the bas-relief on the wall.
Stif: I still wander 'neath porticoes.

The philosophers have typically Greek taste; they love marble, the
pleats of tunics, heady wine, and so forth. Once gestures begin to accom-
pany their dialogue (as they show what noble gestures they prefer), the
dialogue becomes more emotional. Klefiston "becomes heated" and
speaks "with malice" (although he is only talking about grapes) and Stif
becomes even more self-satisfied and proud. He has the last word:
"I lean on an urn", but since there is no urn in sight he leans his elbow
on the back of his hand. Apparently with this he has won the dispute,
for "Klefiston throws (him) an envious look". They exit as slowly as they
have entered, "glancing maliciously at one another", while snakes crawl
from the cistern without any dramatic function whatsoever. The creation
of classical decorum and its subsequent human collapse have been ac-

complished in about ten minutes. The lover of antiquity has his cisterns and pomegranates, and modern man has been entertained by the spectacle of Greeks trying not to act like people.

The play produced most often of all Prutkov's dramatic works is *The Bump-Reader, that is to say the Phrenologist (Čereposlov, sireč' Frenolog)*. It has been staged four times, exactly half the total of Prutkovian dramatic representations.[8] Perhaps its mockery of German quacks and its broad farcial qualities had a wider appeal than the more subtle forms of parody in the other plays.

The source of this "operetta" is a poem given to Vladimir Žemčužnikov by P. P. Eršov in 1854, which subsequently became part of the second scene. The actual author was not Eršov, as Žemčužnikov thought, but N. A. Čižov, a Decembrist,[9] who thus becomes a fifth, if fleeting, contributor to the works of Prutkov (excluding the poets and critics parodied). These vaudeville couplets and the play's subject, which they defined, took place in a past era when enthusiasm for the sciences ran rampant; therefore the play was made out to be written by Petr Fedotyč Prutkov, Koz'ma's father. Luckily the son wrote a preface to his father's work, a masterpiece of the art of the red herring, in which he discusses another work by his father, "Ambition", (which a footnote tells us, has not been found in Koz'ma Prutkov's papers). He even quotes an epigram Sumarokov supposedly wrote against "Ambition":

> Ликуй, парнасский бог! — Прутков уж нынь пиит!
> Для росских зрелищей «Амбицию» чертит!. .
> Хотел он, знать, своей комедией робятской
> Пред светом образец явить амбицьи хватской!
> Но Аполлон за то, собрав *прутков* длинняе,
> Его с Парнасса вон! — чтоб был он поскромняе!

---

[8] *Fantasia* was staged twice and *The Dispute of the Ancient Greek Philosophers* and *The Rash Turk* each once. Nearly all of the eight productions took place in Petersburg. They are, in chronological order: *Fantasia* at the Aleksandrinskij teatr on January 8, 1851; *The Bump-Reader* at the "Veselyj teatr" of N. Evreinov and F. Kommissarževskij in 1909; *Fantasia* there later in the same year; *The Bump-Reader* in the garden theatre "Farce" of Nevolin, also in 1909; *The Dispute of the Ancient Greek Philosophers* in the "Veselyj teatr" in 1911; *The Bump-Reader* in the "Bol'šoj Strel'niskij teatr" by Kurixin in 1911; *The Rash Turk* in the "Krivoe zerkalo" in 1913; and *The Bump-Reader* in Judovskij's theatre in 1922-23. See P. N. Berkov, *Koz'ma Prutkov, direktor probirnoj palatki i poet*, pp. 151-61.

[9] B. Ja. Buxštab, "Koz'ma Prutkov, P. P. Eršov i N. A. Čižov", *Omskij almanax*, V (1945), 116-30.

Rejoice, Parnassian God!—Prutkov is now a bard!
For Russian performance he writes "Ambition"!...
He wished, it seems, with his childish comedy
To provide a model of superlative ambition!
But for this Apollo took some longer "switches",
And chased him from Parnassus, to make him more modest!

This masterful parody of eighteenth-century language and poetic style contains a pun confirming one origin of Prutkov's name: "Apollo took some longer switches ('prutkov')." The parody is worth the whole preface, and the play which follows has a hard time matching it.

The play has three scenes: "The Cranium of the Suitor", "The Ordeal", and "The Promised Husband". The cast of characters are all described by the shape of their skull or the amount and color of their hair. At their head (in more ways than one) is Šiškengol'm, the German phrenologist, "a vigorous but bald old man with a knobby (šiškovatyj) skull". He, his wife, and his marriageable daughter Liza all speak and sing in a macaronic mixture of Russian and German. They also mix metaphors. When their Hamlet-like contemplation of skulls is broken by the visit of would-be suitors, they sing in chorus: "The yoke of fate/has cut the grain of contemplation" (three mixed metaphors in only five Russian words: "Sud'biny gnet/myšlen'ja srezal kolos.") The phrenologist, opposing German science to Russian emotion, refuses to marry his daughter to a man lacking the proper bumps of passion on his skull. In the second scene, one of the suitors, Kasimov, decides to change the shape of things by having an assistant to the phrenologist hit him on his shaven head with a hammer to produce the necessary bumps. In a scene of pure slapstick farce, the victim sings tearfully as each blow of the hammer brings him a new bump of virtue or talent. Fame, music, learning and sensibility rise in lumps on his head, the bump of patience coming last. The phrenologist, however, is still not satisfied with these bumps, and in the last scene a hydropath named Jeronimus-Amalija von Kurcgalop enters to claim Liza's hand, while she eagerly begins to take a curative bath as the curtain falls. Koz'ma Prutkov did well to attribute this play to his father; his own strength was not such slapstick operetta, nor was he ever again to rely on stereotyped notions such as the ones that Germans are quacks and that Russians submit to getting hit, without turning them not into farce but into parody.

The more delicate humor and greater originality of Prutkov's dramatic talents blossomed again in 1863 with the publication of *The Rash Turk*,

or Is it Nice to be a Grandson?, called a "natural conversational representation". Its exact authorship is unknown. Again, its point of departure
is parody, but the parody of one or two individuals gets lost in the general
humor. One admiring critic called it "the most refined parody by Prutkov... and at the same time absurd to the point of impossibility, of
cynicism."[10] In the prologue the writer speaks of the "new word" that
must be brought into Russian literature in the second half of the nineteenth century and of the "purity" and "sincerity" with which he presents
the play to the spectator—all favorite catchwords of Apollon Grigor'ev,
whom Vladimir had taken to task more extensively in "An Impossible
Situation". The "new word" that the cousins ridiculed became a kind of
conversational naturalism in which characters talked at random, as in
life, without advancing the plot of the drama. Tolstoj shunned this in his
own drama and he criticized Ostrovskij for it in a letter to M. M. Stasjulevič (October 7, 1869):

> I can say further, in all sincerity, that I hold sacred the rule precluding the
> introduction into drama of people who speak about the weather and about
> sturgeon, as in Ostrovskij, without any necessity for the movement of the
> drama. I have not put in a single nonfunctional word.[11]

But what Aleksej Tolstoj would never do, Koz'ma Prutkov makes the
subject of an entire play.

In *The Rash Turk* the characters who gather in a widow's salon in
Petersburg to lament the death of Ivan Semenyč bear the same names as
those in *Fantasia*, but they are not by any means the same characters.
In fact they have no character at all that can be deduced from their
conversation. The play totally lacks a plot and its title has nothing to do
with anything until the very end, when the supposedly dead Ivan Semenyč
rushes into the room and announces that the hostess has a Turkish
grandson and that he will tell how he made this important discovery.
But here, a note tells us, "the manuscript unfortunately breaks off and
it is hardly possible to imagine that this extremely remarkable work of
Koz'ma Prutkov was completed by him. Prutkov's editors, like Gogol's
Rudyj Pan'ko, are faced with the hazards of their occupation, but here
the convention of the missing manuscript is mocked; Prutkov simply did
not finish it. Not only does the play lack real characters and a plot, it also
lacks a point.

[10]   Homo Novus A. P. Kugel', "Zametki", *Teatr i iskusstvo*, No. 3 (1913), pp. 66-67.
[11]   *M. M. Stasjulevič i ego sovremenniki v ix perepiske*, II (St. Petersburg, 1912), 336.

Nonetheless, it is remarkably structured upon conversational inanities. The characters preface their *non sequiturs* with "and so" and "while we're talking about", but there is no logical connection between one bit of talk and the next. The dialogue of the play has an almost surrealistic quality in its disconnectedness.[12] The refrain of the play is "And so, our Ivan Semenyč no longer exists! ... Everything that was pleasant about him has disappeared with him." This phrase, reminiscent of Shakespeare,[13] recurs as each cluster of gossip wears itself down, and it rewinds the social mechanism for new conversation. As with Gogol', new characters proliferate in breathlessly recounted anecdotes having nothing to do with the deceased. We learn about Ivan Semenyč only that his career was ruined when he tried to play the violin without rosin (Prutkov had already warned about the importance of rosin in one of his aphorisms). Then someone says that the price of bread is reported to have risen in the Tambov *gubernija*, and the hostess answers: "Speaking of Tambov, how many versts from Moscow to Ryazan and back?" One of the men replies, "I can tell you one way without even looking in the almanac, but back I don't know." At a new mention of the deceased, one guest says:

I knew him! ... We journeyed with him in the mountains of the East and shared amicably the anguish of exile. What a country is the East! ... Imagine: on the right—a mountain; on the left—a mountain; in front, a mountain; but in back, as you yourself may imagine, the rotten West glows dark blue!

Lermontov and the Slavophils have been crushed in one blow. The East reminds the hostess of a dream she had, but Milovidov for some reason begs her not to recount it. Batog-Batyev describes his medicines and promises to show his wounds, "but only after tea".

As this item of interest also reaches a dead end, Milovidov launches into a long description of a dinner given by the deceased. He not only lists every possible variety of food, but Prutkov, while outdoing the naturalists, also adds some bureaucratic grotesqueries of his own:

[12]   As André Breton defined it: "Le surréalisme poétique ... s'est appliqué jusqu'ici à rétablir dans sa vérité absolue le dialogue, en dégageant les deux interlocuteurs des obligations de la politesse. Chacun d'eux poursuit simplement son soliloque, sans chercher à en tirer un plaisir dialectique particulier ... (La réponse) est en principe totalement indifférente à l'amour-propre de celui qui a parlé. Les mots, les images ne s'offrent que comme tremplins à l'esprit de celui qui écoute." André Breton, *Les manifestes du surréalisme* (Paris: Sagittaire, 1946), p. 59.

[13]   Mark Antony's "The good is oft interred with their bones" is a somewhat loftier phrase. Ivan Semenyč had only "the pleasant" to lose.

The culinary roots lying in the soup depicted all the orders adorning the breasts of the personages present ... the little bones in the cutlets were of ivory and they were encased *en papillote*, on which each person read his own rank, life, and age—a compliment!

Sometimes the eye must have been more enchanted than the palate, as when "the cooked fish was served in rose-water", and "For some reason, they didn't serve jam", but in general the feast equals that dreamed up by Xlestakov. It is a peculiarly Prutkovian reverie both in its bureaucratic flamboyance and in his sophisticated creators' full use of their knowledge of *haute cuisine* to crush the poor writer who presumed to put into his play a single nonfunctional sturgeon or a dramatically unmotivated soup.

There is no question about the authorship of Prutkov's only mystery play, *The Affinity of Universal Forces* (*Srodstvo mirovyx sil*). Aleksej Žemčužnikov noted in his diary on September 18, 1883:

> Wrote for Prutkov (now finished it: one in the morning) the mystery play "The Affinity of Universal Forces". 96 verses free and in meter—more of the latter—mixed with prose. I think that Volodin'ka will be content. I'll copy it over and, if I can, send it to him tomorrow.[14]

Vladimir was more than content and included this in the 1884 *Complete Works*. It is different in genre from Prutkov's other works, but completely Prutkovian in spirit. A "mystery in eleven scenes", *The Affinity of Universal Forces* parodies all allegories with a "higher" meaning and especially the structure of the conventional mystery and romantic symbolism à la *Faust*. It is strikingly similar to Stepan Trofimovič's "dangerous" allegory in Dostoevskij's *The Possessed*.[15] It substitutes a romantic hero for Everyman. Instead of telling the usual story of man's Creation, Fall,

---

[14] A. M. Žemčužnikov, Diary "Liza", BiL, Rukopisnyj otdel, Muzejnoe sobranie, Fond 101, No. 4801-4802.

[15] See F. M. Dostoevskij, *Sobranie sočinenij* (Moscow, 1957), VII, 10-11. Stepan Trofimovič's work is described as "some sort of allegory in lyrical-dramatic form, recalling the second part of Faust." It includes "a chorus of incorporeal powers of some sort" and at one point "a mineral, that is, a completely inanimate object, sings about something." A civilized young man in it wants to lose his reason and at the end begins a new life full of new insight. Everything has "a hint of higher meaning". Dostoevskij's description sounds very Prutkovian, but he has also padded it with other things. Žemčužnikov may have read *The Possessed* or, more likely, both works may have a common source of inspiration in the writings of the 1830's. The two works are juxtaposed in part in *Russische literarische Parodien*, ed. Dm. Tschižewskij (Wiesbaden: Otto Harrassowitz, 1957), pp. 31-32.

and Redemption, this mystery relates how a poet remembers his happy childhood, hangs himself, and is miraculously saved. The cast includes:

A smooth valley, a great poet, a high oak, a star of an order, a star of the heavens, a hollow of a tree, an owl, a hillock, a lump of earth, rope, the complete works of the Great Poet, the Northern Aquilon (*sic*), the highest and longest branch, a southern hurricane, a field-mouse, the hours of night, the still of night, the sun beyond the horizon, the sun in the heavens, the world beyond the grave momentarily, a cloak, a small and a large acorn, and the general reunion of universal forces.

Nature is not only personified, but given different roles in different positions, parodying a very primitive (or very modern) symbolism.

Romantic metaphor and attitudes are parodied simply by being brought to life in a kind of comic personification or *realizacija metafory*. For instance, "the valley awakens suddenly" and begins to sing. The poet appears draped in a cloak, and sings a folk song which he interrupts with reminiscences of childhood. But casting aside these happy memories ("No proč',/Nenužnye o detstve vspominan'ja"), he asserts in rather broken syntax and unpoetic diction that he has come to the end of life's path:

и час настал
Мне перейти хоть к грустному, быть может,
Но к верному, бесспорно, результату.

He then salutes the oak and launches into a parody of romantic monologue, with the usual romantic paranoia ("Menja ljudej presleduet vražda"), seeking peace only in the grave, the laurel wreath torn from his brow and the order from his breast. He ends with a mad vision of the world:

Всеобщий бред. . . Всё лезет вон из нормы!. .
Пусть без меня придут: потоп и трус,
Огонь и глад, и прочие реформы!. .

We begin to suspect from the poet's vocabulary that he, like Prutkov, has also served in the bureaucracy. A star shines on the poet and he wonders how to interpret this ("Kak ponimat'?"). Obviously nature is an enigma. Nature is also an indifferent observer; an owl annoys him with its glassy stare. Even the oak is too high to hang himself from and he must stand on his *Complete Works* to reach it with his rope. At this point the North Wind blows onstage, singing of its strength. Nature is both strong and stupid, for the wind unwittingly blows the rope up to the highest branch so the poet can hang himself, which he does. The North Wind goes away but the southern hurricane destroys the oak which dies in stoic resignation and in fewer words than the poet:

> Стоял сто лет. . .
> Пришла кончина!
> Спасенья нет. . .
> Прощай, долина!

The oak falls, saving the poet and killing a field-mouse. Nature's ways are obviously unpredictable. After the storm "the valley is weighed down in silent anguish" and the still of night asks enigmatic questions. The sun rises and forgives the poet his sin. The poet comes to and exclaims that he has managed to see "the undiscover'd country from whose bourn/No traveller returns, as has said Shakespeare William [*sic*: Prutkov followed the Russian habit of putting last names first on official documents, or perhaps he did not know which was the first and which the last name], my gifted colleague."

But the poet, far from being humbled by this miracle, seems to consider it his due. The owl is displaced and the mouse dead, but that is their fate ("Na ix sud'by vziraju xladnokrovno.") Once again the poet can practice his cold indifference on the world. In a final chorus, the general reunion of universal forces echoes this indifference. The comic device of the unchanged person in a world of change has been brought to bear on the figure of the romantic poet, immune even to the death he so passionately seeks. This figure is further developed and parodied in Prutkov's poetry.

Two remaining plays were not published in the *Complete Works* for very different reasons: one was lost and the other was excluded by the editors. The former, *The Triumph of Virtue* (*Toržestvo dobrodeteli*), differs from the other plays in containing more satire than parody; the latter, *Ljubov' and Silin*, is parody of such a diffuse nature that its meaning becomes lost.

Ljubov' i Silin was excluded by Vladimir Žemčužnikov, although it had been published in *Razvlečenie* in 1861. Vladimir's criticism of his brother Aleksandr's play is quite accurate: it lacks both "literary finish" and the "well-known kind of humor"[16] necessary for Prutkov. The play

---

[16] *Supra*, Chap. I, p. 16.

is a grab-bag of Prutkovian tricks, but there is no plot development at all to contain them; they merely float on the surface.

The play takes place on the estate of Silin, a Marshal of the Nobility, during the visit of a Spanish couple named Don Merzavec and Oslabella This gives the author an occasion for many polylinguistic puns, and for a general parody of everything Spanish as seen through Russian eyes, but the idea of the Spaniards adrift in Russia, essentially a good one, is not really developed.[17] The names Merzavec and Oslabella, meaning "a scoundrel" and "she grew weak" (from oslabet', with a Spanish ending) are as successfully suggestive as any Prutkovian names, but very little is done with their meanings. They neither label the characters, nor contradict them, as in *Fantasia*.

The entire play is based on a series of small jokes which are not developed. It opens on a garden scene with "very many flies; Silin eats noodle-soup". After a long silence he speaks; he is an ignorant but ambitious nobleman learning French for self-improvement: "Gom-čelovek. Gam-duša." He also speaks of "vseobščaja ljubov'" (all-embracing love) and his serf girl friend who just happens to be named Ljubov' says she is his love and not all-embracing. He catches a lady-bug on her neck. The two Spaniards who have lost their compass and strayed into the north enter and occasion further puns ("ja Oslabella ne tol'ko s dorogi, no i s roždenija") and some lines reminiscent of Puškin and Lermontov are spoken in a rather contrived context. At the end of Act I the general's widow Kislozvezdova, characterized as "dumb but lascivious", enters with a lantern in her hand and looks lasciviously at Don Merzavec. In Act II, at night, Silin has fallen in love with Oslabella. These various passions are made unPrutkovianly explicit. Prutkovian official language is used, but to no real point, when Silin reads a document concerning the widow. The best part of the act is a bit of pure farce in which the widow carries off Don Merzavec on her shoulders. The decor of Act III mentions more insects, includes a storm and a song, and ends with a voice from the ravine urging everyone to fall on his knees. Nothing has happened except that someone's true identity has been revealed. To provide continuity, Don Merzavec takes a lady-bug from Ljubov's neck, while Silin says "(aside) Two days ago I placed it there."

Ljubov' and Silin proves one thing negatively: if dramatic consistency is to be spoofed, it must be spoofed consistently. In this play there is not a single thread to follow and as a result the reader merely loses interest.

---

[17] The play does not seem to refer specifically to any of the current "Spanish" translations and plays of Rostopčina, Sul'e, Tarnovskij or Longinov.

Characters are not clearly delineated, but merely act as straight men for an impending joke, so that even clever jokes seem forced. The humor of the set-up joke is always slightly embarrassing.

There exist several strands of satiric potential in *Ljubov'* and *Silin*. One is the character of Silin himself, the proud but ignorant Russian nobleman. He tries to read foreign journals and is genuinely disturbed: "They say that foreigners have begun to write much about our beloved fatherland; who else will be in condition to translate for the nobles all that is printed about them?" His drive for self-enlightenment is tinged with paranoia, but a similar fear is apparently shared by his fellow-nobles who accuse him of insulting them by contemplating marriage with the foreigner Oslabella and trying "to betray the fatherland by giving her a map of our city".

The Triumph of Virtue, on the whole more satirical than the other plays, fully equals them in quality. It had been censored for presentation on stage, evidently in 1864, and subsequently lost. Vladimir had hoped to include it in the *Complete Works*, but never found it. He mentions its title in letters as *The Minister of Fertility*, referring to a central figure in the play.[18] The play was first published in *Literaturnoe nasledstvo* in 1959, thus completing Prutkov's works to what would have been the satisfaction of his creators. In a preface to the play written in 1864, the authors claim to be some of the numerous descendants of the deceased Prutkov who communicated with them from the other world "by means of tables and dishes" through spirits. The two who set down his words are said to be the same ones who wrote *Fantasia*—meaning that the authors of *The Triumph of Virtue* are Aleksej Žemčužnikov and Aleksej Tolstoj.

Tolstoj's authorship can be further established by textual evidence. Some of the situations and phrases in the play (for instance the liberal-sounding reactionary who tells his victim he is "a second father" to him) and the frightening quality of higher officialdom as well as its hypocrisy, would, as we have seen, be used by Tolstoj even more sharply in "The Dream of Popov", written almost a decade later.[19] Indeed, the play serves almost as an illustration of Tolstoj's opinion of bureaucrats, expressed in 1851 to his future wife—"people who, under the pretext that they

---

[18] See especially the letter to A. N. Pypin of February 24, 1884: *Koz'ma Prutkov*, p. 401.

[19] This point was made by B. Ja. Buxštab, "Toržestvo dobrodeteli", *Literaturnoe nasledstvo*, LXVIII (1959), 763.

serve, live by intrigues one filthier than the next."[20] The dramatic illustration is both suspenseful and comic, ironic and farcical.

The play has the added dimension of being written by Prutkov, who frets over externals, caring that his characters, officials of high rank, should be proper even when they are dishonest. The title, like the play's development, is therefore ironic. Not virtue, but the most skillful hypocrite of all triumphs at the end.

The plot's suspense hinges upon the successive unfolding of "intrigues one filthier than the next"; in each scene a different character shows his hand and is rapidly ruined by the person he trusted most. The play takes place in Paris, and purports to be a scene from "contemporary French life". What is distant in space can be closer in time. The satire, implicitly directed at contemporary Russia, also reflects actual conditions in Napoleon III's France, where sham liberalism and fake patriotism had been portrayed by Victor Hugo for over a decade.

In Act I De Lageron'er[21] relies upon his secretary Gjugel' to help him obtain the post of Minister of Fertility. Gjugel' has informed him that the current minister cares only about a person's health. "The smallest pimple on the lip" evokes his suspicion. In other words, the minister makes a point of judging people externally and his whole ministry runs on this principle. De Lageron'er writes to the minister parroting these sentiments, and decides for good measure to take a bath in bran to improve his skin. Gjugel', alone onstage, proclaims his intent to sabotage his master's aspirations. The second act takes us higher in rank to the minister himself who, it seems, wants someone innocuous to take his post so that he can control it and at the same time aim for the job of Minister of Health: "I'll dump Fertility on his shoulders and grab for Health!" Having received the letter, he decides to see if De Lageron'er is the right man, when Bienintensionne, seemingly full of good intentions, walks in. He speaks in a mixture of smooth phrases and veiled threats, and the minister dares not oppose him. He produces a sort of blackmail trump card, the first line of a poem written by the minister when he was seventeen: "Golden freedom, the ideal of the nations." The minister disowns this bit of sedition and mutters his hatred of Bienintensionne who kisses him loudly several times, as the two shake hands in an out-

---

[20] *Supra*, Chap. I, p. 2.
[21] His name is taken from that of a French senator under Napoleon III, but he apparently stands for Valuev, Minister of the Interior from 1861 to 1868, who opposed the Russian plans for reform of the fifties, and in 1863 wrote a project for a constitution. See *Ko'zma Prutkov*, p. 454.

ward show of great affection. In the third act, Bienintensionne meets Gjugel', who confides to him his own desires to take the post of Deputy Minister of Fertility. After Bienintensionne has promised to be a "second father" to him, Gjugel' declares with mock patriotism: "I will place everything on the altar of the fatherland!" In the last act, Gjugel' prepares a bath of red peppers and acid for his master. Prutkov adds a footnote that the actor need not undress entirely for this scene for "on stage it would be improper."

There follows a scene partly of farce, like the hammer scene in *The Bump-Reader*, and partly of swift dramatic surprises. De Lageron'er is surprised in the middle of his bath by the visit of the Minister who barges right in, punning that it is pleasant for him to see a subordinate in a lather at the job ("mne prijatno videt' podčinennogo v myle!") and proceeding to ask the naked man his "view on things". De Lageron'er manages to give the right answers, and then leaps out of the bath to embrace the Minister (behind a screen set up by Gjugel'), who protests violently. At this moment Bienintensionne walks in, excusing himself in his usual polite way for not having had himself announced. De Lageron'er is blamed for being naked in his own bathroom. As De Lageron'er is undone, Bienintensionne shows his hand against the Minister as well. He has given the seditious poem to the Ministry of Suspicion and has captured for himself both the Ministries of Health and of Fertility. Even Gjugel' is left out as the winner takes all. Bienintensionne reveals his further good intentions: "You are all freethinkers, therefore all your names will be taken down, but this does not prevent us from remaining on friendly terms."

Once again order is restored at the end of a Prutkov play. But in this play the comic devices, verbal and farcical, are subordinated to a larger theatrical purpose. Not only do hypocrisy and careerism prevail in the higher echelons of the bureaucracy, but the sweet phrases of politeness and the almost liturgical praise of the fatherland also cover up denunciations and back-stabbings. In a world of ministries, Fertility and Health are ruled by Suspicion. Vice steeped in decorum has much comic potential, but some of the speeches strike a serious note. Gjugel' the dangerous lackey says: "I maintain that there is no state on earth freer than ours which, enjoying liberal political institutions, obeys as well the slightest indication of power." The cousins proved themselves masters of left-handed praise, and their good left hand was Koz'ma Prutkov.

Only *The Triumph of Virtue* presents onstage the world of the bureaucracy. The order on the romantic breast, cast off in *The Affinity of Univer-*

sal Forces, is but a minor trademark of Prutkov. While Prutkov himself may be distant from the plays, he still fills them with his trademarks, great and small—the passion for propriety, conversational or bodily competition for a place in the world, words which pour out in torrents of meaningless purposefulness. In the plays, abundant variety of genre, settings and characters often conceals these similarities. In the rest of his prose Prutkov explains himself more fully than in the plays. What were mere trademarks then appear more like obsessions.

IV

THE PROSE:

KOZ'MA PRUTKOV AND THE READER

Koz'ma Prutkov, revelling in his dual role as bureaucrat and poet, is obsessed with explaining himself to the reader. In his works his manner fluctuates as greatly as his vocation. His tone ranges from benignly condescending in some aphorisms to ominously imposing in his project. As a bureaucrat he is stern, as a poet proud, and, as a literal and figurative nobody in either case, comic. In his poetry he may have tended to let himself drift into the heady lyrical spheres; in his prose he tended toward heavier, non-fictional genres—epistolary, autobiographical, historical, aphoristic, polemical and pedagogical. Thus, nearly all his works have an explanatory tone; and with Koz'ma Prutkov, an explanation usually becomes a self-explanation.

Prutkov's prosaic voice was first heard in *The Contemporary* in a preface to his *Leisure Musings*, the first of many prefaces to his works and one already containing many Prutkovian traits. The preface is dated "April 11, 1853 (annus, i)", a date which would became one of Prutkov's favorites. Nearly all his works are dated on the eleventh of some month, and the year is given in Latin in the nominative and genitive, the school-book or dictionary forms which Prutkov obviously had memorized. As Prutkov explained in "From the Other World", "my love for classic-ism always expressed itself almost uniquely by the word 'annus, i' placed after my works; but is this really so little? Indeed, at that time classicism was not in such good repute as now...". The preface is ad-dressed to the reader; in fact, the word *čitatel'* insistently precedes nearly every paragraph. Often Prutkov calls upon a larger audience—*čelovek*!, man himself—but he never writes for himself alone. With the self-con-fidence of a Renaissance humanist, he proclaims, "I want glory. Glory consoles mankind." In short, beginning with his first words Prutkov speaks the unspeakable. His charm lies in his naiveté. Freud wrote:

The naive occurs if someone completely disregards an inhibition because it is not present in him—if, therefore, he appears to overcome, it without any effort. It is a condition for the naive's producing its effect that we should know that the person concerned does not possess the inhibition; otherwise we call him not naive but impudent. We do not laugh at him, but are indignant at him.[1]

As we have seen in the reviews of *Fantasia*, Prutkov did make some critics indignant, for the very existence of his work seemed a purposeless impudence. Other critics, however, such as Grigor'ev and Družinin, did not fail to appreciate in Prutkov a purposeful purposelessness, which is nowhere more evident than in his prose.

Prutkov claims in his first preface to have written "from childhood", and to have "much unfinished (d'inaché)". One of his poses is that of the careless artist who leaves scraps of poems forgotten in half-finished notebooks. This parodies the Romantic device of sketchiness, focusing on some things while leaving others "unsaid". Prutkov started writing poetry because he "became convinced, reading others, that if they are poets, then so am I." In an epistle published in 1859 and addressed to an "unknown *feuilleton* writer" he disclaims any parodic (critical or humorous) intent:

I merely analyzed in my mind the majority of poets enjoying success; that analysis led me to a synthesis. ... Having desired glory, I took the surest road to it: *imitation* of precisely those poets who had already acquired it. Do you hear?—"imitation" and not parody!

He disparagingly refers to the feuilletonist's article as a "statejka", (the diminutive pejorative form of the word *stat'ja*) and characteristically, he writes an explanatory footnote to the epistle. Even his private polemics must be elucidated for his readers.

Eventually Prutkov's creators thought it necessary to supply additional facts about Prutkov, but these facts had a tendency to multiply, so that it is difficult to determine the "true" fiction. The approved versions of Prutkov's biography, those mentioned in the *Complete Works*, include the "Biographical Facts about Koz'ma Prutkov" and the "Short Necrology". Aleksandr Žemčužnikov wrote on his own "Some Materials for the Biography of Koz'ma Prutkov", but the facts therein were not recognized by Vladimir. Aleksandr's work takes the form of an autobiography, and includes as its best touch a report card in which the

---

[1] Sigmund Freud, *Jokes and Their Relation to the Unconscious*, trans. James Strachey (New York: W. W. Norton and Co., 1963), p. 182.

subjects learned by Prutkov are all qualified by different adverbs indicating
Prutkov's success and the ingenuity of his teacher: "uspešno", "ot duši",
"silno-živo-xorošo", "udovletvoritel'no", "smelo-otčetlivo", "razumno-
ponjatno", "nazidatel'no prepoxval'no". ("Successfully", "from the
soul", "powerfully, animatedly good", "satisfactory", "boldly intelli-
gible", "rationally understandable", "edifyingly praiseworthy".) This parodies a much-used grading system and, indeed, the very idea of grading.
But Aleksandr's autobiography appears less successful than the biographical form used by Vladimir. This is due in part to Vladimir's greater
talent, and in part to a stylistic factor. When Prutkov wrote in an imper-
sonal literary genre, that of biography, he could make his personal
trademarks stand out in sharper relief. The humor derives in part from
this double layer—the known literary form and the new Prutkovian use
of it. In fictional autobiography, the two tend to mesh indistinguishably,
since the form itself allows for individual variations. If one of these
styles, a known type of autobiography, were parodied, it would not be
Prutkov's own story. In fictional biography, however, Vladimir was able
to preserve a double level—one of the Prutkovian "facts" and one of
the official, serious tone of the biographies of important people, as it
might have appeared in the official press. Once again, parody, no matter
how vaguely felt, adds to the enjoyment of the work.

The "Biographical Facts", written in 1883, superseded the "Short
Necrology" published nearly twenty years earlier. The necrology, supposedly written by a nephew of Prutkov, gives more personal details of
his life: Prutkov married young and left behind his inconsolable widow
plus four daughters and six sons. The nephew even alludes to the marri-
ageability of the daughters. Prutkov died "after long suffering" and left
a word to the public to cherish his memory "with a heartfelt tear".The
tone of the "Necrology" is less humorous, because more personal than
that of the "Biographical Facts". These begin:

Koz'ma Petrovič Prutkov spent all his life, except the years of childhood
and early boyhood, in government service: first the military and then the civil.
He was born on the eleventh of April, 1803; he died on the thierteenth of
January, 1863.

Already a dry factual tone may be discerned, but the facts become more
fantastic. "In 1820 he entered the military service only for the full-dress
uniform." At that time an extraordinary event in his life occurred; he
had a dream (on the eleventh of April, of course). The dream, a parody
of a Freudian dream *avant la lettre*, follows:

He saw before him a naked brigadier general in epaulettes who, having pulled him from his cot without letting him dress, led him silently along some long and dark corridors to the top of a high and sharply crowned hill, and there before him began to pull out various precious materials from an ancient vault, showing them to him one after another and even putting some of them on his chilled body. With bewilderment and fear Prutkov awaited the outcome of this puzzling event; but suddenly when the most costly of these materials touched him, he felt on his whole body a strong electric shock, from which he awoke all in perspiration. It is not known what meaning Koz'ma Petrovič Prutkov gave to that dream.

Thus speaks the official biographer. With the help of modern psychology (which Prutkov's tutors obviously foresaw) we might determine that Prutkov underwent a dream of sexual desire (note the long, dark corridors and the shape of the hill) with an anxiety-producing authority figure or possibly even homosexual ramifications (the naked brigadier general in epaulettes, i.e., wearing his rank but not his clothes) followed by swift punishment in the form of castration at the very moment of attainment. This interpretation of the dream is confirmed by the fact that Prutkov, greatly shaken, left the army on the very next day forever. He joined the Ministry of Finances, where he worked in the Assay Office *(probirnaja palatka)* and remained there for the rest of his life, finally becoming its director and receiving the Order of St. Stanislav of the First Degree. The Assay Office actually existed (although it had no directors and was not part of the Ministry of Finances) in St. Petersburg and Moscow for the testing and stamping of gold and silver. Thus Prutkov could be a big a fish in a small pond, and presumably could still touch precious materials without fear. His dream, loaded with fictitious significance, may be either a parody of literary dreams, highly consequential, but uninterpreted by a reluctant narrator, or one of dreams in general. In any case it works beautifully to explain Prutkov's presence both in the army (where he would have to have written his "military aphorisms") and his sudden switch to civil life.

In the civil service, only the reforms disturbed Prutkov's contentment. He countered them with his own projects, declaring himself "an enemy of all so-called questions"—a phrase which recurs in his works and appears in one of Aleksej Tolstoj's satires as well.[2] Thus, Prutkov had the heart of a conservative and loved his important-sounding sinecure. Including his time as a hussar, he served for more than forty years, but "on the literary scene acted publicly only five years (in 1854 and in the

---

[2] In a satiric epistle to F. M. Tolstoj, Aleksej wrote in 1869: Ja ž drug vlastej i večnyj vrag tak nazyvaemyx voprosov!

early 1860's)". As we have seen, the biographer claims that only his guardians or "false friends" first encouraged him to publish and made him bold and trenchant, without, however, adding anything to his personality that was not already latent in it.

The figure of Koz'ma Prutkov, separated from his writings, is undoubtedly satiric. His biographer writes: "In this respect (i.e., in his self-confidence) he was a child of his times, distinguished by self-confidence and disregard of obstacles". Vladimir Žemčužnikov saw it as an epoch where fools rushed in with projects and were rewarded with medals, where superfluity was superfluously recognized. Ivanov-Razumnik called Prutkov a typical and inevitable result of (his) epoch, which he characterized as "an epoch of official Philistinism".[3] Vladimir Žemčužnikov would have considered this a one-sided explanation, as he wrote in a letter of February 27, 1883, to A. N. Pypin, using many phrases from the biography:

> It is remarkable that in Prutkov there existed simultaneously both these forms of self-satisfaction and decisiveness; but it is not known whether this came from the varied richness of his nature or whether in the society of his time both these forms did not exist, only not in the degree to which they always do.[4]

Vladimir probably was affirming both possibilities.

Prutkov definitely resembles the great anti-social comic figures in Bergson's famous definition:

> Comedy begins ... with what might be called a growing callousness to social life. Any individual is comic who automatically goes his own way without troubling himself about getting into touch with the rest of his fellow beings.[5]

As we have seen in Chapter I, Prutkov seems to be saying, "Everything human is foreign to me." Thus his relation to the reader, however insistent, has an air of unreality. Alternately his tone becomes commanding or patronizing—in the "Forewarning" ("Preduvedomlenie") he speaks with the reader "like a father with his son". Most of the time he appears merely arbitrary, with the sublime arbitrariness of a being who considers himself superior. He appears as a great inhuman, antisocial type, more specifically a bureaucratic type, and only secondarily a Russian bureaucrat of the mid-nineteenth century.

---

[3] P. V. Ivanov-Razumnik, *Istorija russkoj obščestvennoj mysli* (Petersburg, 1907), I, 155.
[4] Koz'ma Prutkov, p. 399.
[5] Henri Bergson, "Laughter", in *Comedy*, ed. Wylie Sypher (New York: Doubleday and Co., 1956), p. 147.

Prutkov, remote from humanity and at the same time trying to instruct it, produces such comic didactic works as the "Alphabet for children", the aphorisms, the "Historical Materials" and the "Project". The "Alphabet for Children" is perhaps Aleksandr's best contribution to Prutkov's works. Vladimir wrote "Saša's foolishness" (glupost' Sašin'-kina) on a copy of it,[6] but a later critic came closer to the mark when he wrote about the alphabet: "Terrible nonsense, but one cannot quite say, 'How stupid!' "[7]

An alphabet for children is supposed to help the children learn the letters in order. Even Lear's "Nonsense Alphabets" have rhyme and tell a story. Prutkov's, however, have neither rhyme nor reason and obstruct any logical learning process. The "Alphabet for Children" may be a parody of a serious alphabet with lofty moral-religious aims. I. A. Sukiasova has a strong argument when she cites as the "indisputable source" of Prutkov's alphabet the *Novaja i polnaja russkaja azbuka (New and Complete Russian Alphabet)* written in 1854 by D. N. Šarapov, which has the same absurd choice of examples. For instance, "Ž—živaja ryba ('live fish'). Z—Zlobnye krendeli" ('wicked rolls').[8] Prutkov too uses the adjective rather than the noun to illustrate his letter: "C—Celoe jabloko" ('a whole apple'), and often his noun is lexically as well as grammatically more memorable than his adjective. Prutkov has other original touches: "Ž—Žitejskoe more" ('the sea of life': a reference to one of his poems); "T—Tatarin, prodajuščij mylo ili xalaty" ('a Tartar selling soap or bathrobes': not only a reference to a character in *Fantasia*, but also humorous because of its relative length); "U—Učitel' tance-vanija i logiki" ('a teacher of dancing and logic': the conjunction "and" links two unlikely subjects); "D—Djunkirxen gorod" ('Dunkirk town': a foreign city illustrates a Russian alphabet). The overall order of the alphabet itself has no logical continuity: "A—Anton kozu vedet" ('Anton leads the goat'); "B—Bol'naja Julija" ('Sick Julia'). Thus, not just the separate units but even the entire alphabet works against any instructive purpose.

As an aphorist, Prutkov instructs an even larger audience, all mankind, and does so even more authoritatively. As Vladimir said in the February 27 letter to Pypin:

---

[6] Koz'ma Prutkov, p. 455.
[7] A. V. Amfiteatrov, "Koz'ma Prutkov v *Iskre*", *Zabytyj smex* (Moscow, 1914), I, 436.
[8] I. A. Sukiasova, *Jazyk i stil' parodij Koz'my Prutkova* (Tbilisi, 1961), p. 93.

Such a relationship (of authority) to his readers ... expresses itself above all in the aphorisms, in the "fruits of meditation." Sometimes he actually ponders and then utters not admonition or advice, but an order, a command. ...[9]

Nevertheless, Prutkov's commands always take Prutkovian forms. As the "Biographical Facts" state:

The majority of his aphorisms either say with self-importance "bureaucratic" trivialities *(kazennye pošlosti)*, or forcefully smash through open doors, or speak forth thoughts which not only have no relation to his time and country, but are also located as it were outside any time and place whatsoever.

Their absurdity and their timelessness have won them a certain renown separate from that of Prutkov's other works.

No part of Koz'ma Prutkov's works is better known than his aphorisms. If the genre had not already existed, Prutkov would have had to invent it, for it was an ideal mode in which to express his cautious conservatism as sententiously as possible. As one critic defined it,"The proverb is a secular or purely human oracle ... its authority comes from experience: for it, wisdom is the tried and tested way; only folly seeks what is new, and the essential virtues are prudence and moderation."[10] Prutkov's aphorisms can be and are used by any Russian in any situation. They are used ironically, i.e., in the spirit in which they were written, and straightforwardly, thereby giving them a double irony. They are quoted correctly, incorrectly, and often pseudocorrectly, when the author knows that to use a Prutkovism suffices to set a tone of levity.

Prutkovian aphorisms stem from a general human desire to ridicule the proverbs one has been forced to swallow from childhood—the folk sayings reduced to bourgeois practicality. Who has not said ironically that "honesty is the best policy" or "idle hands are the Devil's workshop"? But Prutkov's tutors chose a different tactic altogether. Some of their proverbs are stolen from journals and plays of the day (especially Nos. 1, 85, 111). One, "Zeal Conquers All" (No. 84) was stolen directly from an inscription on a golden medal of honor of a certain count P. A. Klejnmixel', a man close to Tsar Nicholas I, who in 1838 had rapidly fulfilled the task of reconstructing the Winter Palace after the fire. Judging from the triumphant motto, one might think that the count rebuilt the Palace with his own hands. But most of Prutkov's aphorisms

---

[9] Koz'ma Prutkov, p. 402.
[10] Northrop Frye, *Anatomy of Criticism* (New York: Athenaeum, 1966), p. 298.

derive their humor from being completely original by being completely obvious, outdoing their peers in lack of wit.

In the West, some of the greatest philosophers and writers of the seventeenth and eighteenth centuries exercised their minds by composing aphorisms. The best maxims of this age were written by La Rochefoucauld. He scrupulously avoided the double pitfalls of banality and obscurity; he is never too obvious and never too *recherché*. His choice of metaphor is so apt that it seems to spring from the thought itself. A constant pessimism informs his sayings; the major wisdom they impart is the cultivation of self-perfection, being honest with oneself. Because they seem to be directed to himself as much as to other men. La Rochefoucauld's maxims never lapse into sententiousness.

In the nineteenth century the art of the maxim was in decline. It had lost both the earthy pungency of the peasant and the polished self-examination of the aristocrat, and had not yet been revived by the fresh cynicism of Oscar Wilde or the pseudo-country naiveté of Max Beerbohm. Still, in Russia, aphorisms ran rampant in the journals of the day.[11] Their sentimentality (for example, about the sweet inevitability of love) was surpassed only by their sententious obviousness—and in the latter they were worthy of Prutkov. Furthermore, writing aphorisms was a favorite pastime of the educated gentleman bureaucrat that Prutkov aspired to be.[12]

If an aphorism is not original, if it does not succeed in piercing a small hole in the obvious, it has no reason to exist. Prutkov's conscious sententiousness was quite original at the time. He did not merely puncture the over-inflated; he blew it up until it burst of its own accord. This tactic worked better in some instances than in others. Vladimir Žemčužnikov, with his usual good taste, omitted many of the aphorisms which had appeared in *Literaturnyj eralaš* and *Iskra* from the *Complete Works* of 1884. Often he revised the journal versions, usually for the better, and arranged them differently, giving each a number.

Prutkov compulsively makes sure that the reader understands his metaphors, no matter how hackneyed they are. He reminds us that the bark, travelling on the river of time, is "none other than man" (2). His

---

[11] The journal *Literaturnaja gazeta* had a special section for sayings and anecdotes. See Sukiasova, pp. 88-89, for quotations of some of these.
[12] See the "Mysli i zamečanija Grafa Bludova", in E. P. Kovalevskij, *Sobranie sočinenij*, (St. Petersburg, 1871), I, 257-77. The aphoristic remarks of Count Bludov (1785-1864), an enlightened conservative who served as Minister of the Interior and Head of the Second Section, have the same pompous intonation, the same structure of the rhetorical question and exclamation as those of Prutkov.

similes, inapt but not inept, may liken a weakening memory to a fading
forget-me-not (12). His most famous admonitions are indisputable: "No
one can embrace the unembraceable" (3, 67, 104); "Look at the root"
(5); and "Be vigilant!" (42—"Bdi"—the shortest work in Russian literature). Prutkov lovingly repeats them in his other works. He proposes
easy solutions for life's greatest ills. To the ugly, he says: "If you want to
be handsome, join the Hussars" (16). To the unhappy: "If you want to
be happy, be so!" (80). Everything is for the best: "Death is placed at
the end of life so that it can be prepared for most conveniently" (34);
"Nails and hairs are given to man in order to provide him with a cont-
inual, but light, occupation" (71). Extremes should be avoided: "The man
wishing to dine too late risks dining next morning" (36). Almost reassuring
are the words, "Don't be timid before the enemy: man's most fearful
enemy is himself" (59). And it is consoling to find, several maxims later,
that "Even oysters have enemies" (86).

Occasionally the aphorisms have a pseudo-Oriental tone: "By hours
is measured time, and by time the life of man; but by what, pray, do you
measure the depth of the Eastern ocean?" (62) and "Where is the beginning of that end with which the beginning is ended?" (78). But, unlike
the mystic, Prutkov usually has an answer to problems of existence; very
often they are tinged with his characteristic romanticism, bureaucratism,
or propriety: "The official dies, and his decorations remain on the face
of the earth" (21);[13] "In the depth of every breast is its serpent" (88);
"Only in government service do you learn to know truth" (89); "Do not
joke with women; these jokes are stupid and improper" (91). Prutkov
was always concerned with propriety. Occasionally one hears the voices
of Tolstoj and the Žemčužnikovs. They could not resist: "A specialist is
like a swollen cheek: his fullness is one-sided" (101).

Most of the aphorisms that depend on puns for their humor were
eliminated. The best maxims are based not on verbal wit (which Prutkov
lacked) but on sheer illogic. At their best, they have the gentle charm of
"If you have a fountain, turn it off; even a fountain needs a rest" (22).
(Could this refer to the fountain of maxim-making?) "Even turpentine
is useful for something" (60); what is it, if not useful? It also sounds in
Russian like the word for patience (terpentin/terpenie). "I do not fully
understand why many people call fate a turkey, and not some other bird
more similar to fate" (149), he ingenuously asks. Finally, he states con-
fidently that "A good cigar is like the globe: it turns for the contentment

---

[13]   Not in the *Complete Works*.

of man" (155). Whether or not a cigar necessarily turns ("vertitsja") is irrelevant.

The aphorisms repeat each other in theme, in metaphor, and even in toto.[14] Prutkov obviously felt it was better to make a point several times than to state it just once, no matter how absurd this practice might appear. As one critic said of the aphorisms, "their distinguishing feature lies in their complete absurdity and in an almost pathological senselessness.[15]

The "Military Aphorisms" and "Ceremonial" (the full title is "Ceremonial pogrebenija tela v boze usopšego poručika i kavalera Faddeja Koz'miča P. . . . . .") form an expansion to the aphorisms. They are written in very prosaic couplets, with uneven meter and inexact rhyme. Both Vladimir Žemčužnikov and Aleksej Tolstoj served in the army in 1855, but stylistically these works bear the mark of Tolstoj, especially because of the unusual rhymes and foreign words he liked to use in his own poetry. "Ceremonial" has the extremely Tolstoyan couplet:"Idut slavjanofily i nigilisty; U tex i u drugix nogti ne čisty." ('The Slavophiles and Nihilists go forth; neither these nor those have clean nails.') We have already seen his somewhat aristocratic distaste for both Slavophiles and Nihilists.

"Ceremonial" may have been written first. It mentions events of the early sixties, whereas the aphorisms refer to occurrences of the late seventies and early eighties. Buxštab suggests that it parodies the ceremonial burial of Nicholas I.[16] In any case neither work was included in the Complete Works for reasons of censorship. They were first published in their entirety by N. L. Brodskij in 1922.[17] Their military content sets them apart from Prutkov's other works, but in style they are unmistakably Prutkovian. Their form itself defies logic. "Ceremonial", an absurd procession in which various incompatible Russians march together, consists of couplets strung together in somewhat illogical sequence. The "Military" aphorisms contain separate and absurdly epigrammatic vignettes of army life.

The aphorisms have as dubious heroes two soldiers named Glazenap and Butenop; such names actually existed—the Glazenaps were a famous noble and military family in Russia in the first half of the nineteenth century ("glazenapy" also means "peepers"—slang for eyes), and the

---

[14] "Nikto ne obnimet neob'jatnogo" is repeated five times.
[15] Koz'ma Prutkov, Proizvedenija ne vošedšie v sobranie sošinenij, p. 18.
[16] Koz'ma Prutkov, p. 442.
[17] Golos minuvšego, No. 2 (1922).

Butenops had a house in Moscow, not far from the Žemčužnikovs, which first boasted a clock on its roof.[18] The names illustrate the traditional German presence in the Russian army, but they also provide in aphorism 41 (consisting of thirty-two lines, rather long for an aphorism) a wonderful series of chain rhymes, because the syllables "nap" and "nop" rhyme with a great variety of purely Russian words, including one prudently left unstated by Prutkov.

In fact, the purpose of the military aphorisms seems to be the rhyme itself, and not their stated "application and understanding" by officers and lower ranks. For example, they are told that "Not for any old Anjuta/are salutes made from cannons." Anjuta is dragged in because her name rhymes with salutes ("Anjuty"/"saljuty") or perhaps vice versa. Similarly, we find the rhymes "akacii/dislokacii", "odekolony/kolonny" determining an absurd context. Sometimes the rhyme is made out of a line of pure nonsense ("Aj, firli-fit' tjurlja-tjutju") rare in Prutkov's work, but common is soldiers' songs of the day.[19] Often the rhyme itself is purposefully inexact: (popu/pupu, Evropa/šljapa), providing both variety and a hint of military clumsiness.

The aphoristic couplets often have a tone of satire: "All my men are dressed in proper uniforms; why should I worry about food?" or of insubordination (the commander's baldness is referred to). "Ceremonial" lumps together and outspokenly condemns "Russian atheism and orthodoxy". Such outrageous statements invite comment and Prutkov's creators provided a built-in critic in the form of a regimental commander who adorns the aphorisms with his own footnotes, remarking usually disparagingly on both their form and content. His comments range from "this goes without saying" to "this is written directly against me" to "a bad rhyme" to "in this aphorism I don't see anything military" to "this is stolen from me" to "who are these people anyway?" The footnotes heap ridiculous comment upon ridiculous content, but they harmonize perfectly with the Prutkovian passion for accuracy and for propriety. The regimental commander is obviously an alter-ego of the *Fantasia* censor and of Prutkov himself. In his *Works*, Prutkov and his sub-narrators comment on everything, no matter how trivial, and always from a self-righteous and occasionally paranoid point of view. Prutkov's creators satirized the institutions of mid-nineteenth century Russia by showing the paranoid element as well as the sycophancy in the patriotism they inspired.

[18]   Koz'ma Prutkov, ed. P. N. Berkov, pp. 562-63.
[19]   Koz'ma Prutkov, pp. 440-41.

"The Historical Materials of Fedot Kuz'mic Prutkov (grandfather)" uses another Prutkovian sub-narrator, his grandfather. These "materials", really a series of quasi-historic anecdotes each about a paragraph long, are presented to the reader by Prutkov himself as "Excerpts from the Notes of my Grandfather". In their preface he elucidates their origin in a bit of Prutkovian scholarship: "My grandfather was born in 1720 and finished the notes in 1780; therefore, they were begun in 1764." Similar dates and facts precede the foreword by the old man himself. The language of the entire work represents the eighteenth century at its most barbaric, with interminable sentences the length of an entire paragraph.

Уподобляяся, под вечер жизни моей, оному древних римлян Цынцынатусу, в гнетомые старостью года свои утешаюсь я, в деревенской тихости, кроткими наслаждениями и изобретенными удовольствиями; и достохвально в воспоминаниях упражняяся, тебе, сынишке моему, Петрушке, ради душевныя пользы и научения, жизненного прохождения моего описание и многие гисторические, из наук и светских разговоров почерпнутые, сведения после гроба моего оставить положил.

Likening myself, in the evening of my life, to that ancient Roman Cincinnatus, in years oppressed by old age, I console myself, in the quiet of the country, with mild pleasures and ingenious satisfactions; and in praiseworthy fashion exercising myself in reminiscences, to you, Petruška sonny, for the sake of spiritual usefulness and learning, this description of my life's journey and much historical information drawn from learning and social conversation, have I resolved to leave after my death.

The modern Russian, when attempting to read these sentences aloud, becomes lost in them and begins to get the cases mixed up. To Prutkov's creators must be given credit for following through with the correct ones.

As the preface states, the historical materials are drawn "from learning and society conversations"; they contain a blend of pseudo-fact, Prutkovian historical name-dropping, and historical small-talk. They may be named jokingly after a section of the contemporary journal *Moskvitjanin*[20] and they may contain frequent references to contemporary figures, but the "Historical Materials" chiefly parody what Vladimir Solov'ev called "the 'remarkable events' *(dostoprimečatelnosti)* of eighteenth-century sborniki ... (with) the peculiar mixture of triteness and absurd-

[20] P. N. Berkov, *Koz'ma Prutkov, direktor Probirnoj palatki i poet*, p. 86.

ity in the context of such stories."[21] Dostoevskij in "Winter Remarks on Summer Impressions" tries to recreate the reader of such stories which he remembers looking at in his youth and remarks: "What a naive faith they had then in the seriousness and indispensability of such European news."[22] Koz'ma Prutkov still sees importance in such items and passes them on to his readers.

Dostoevskij analyzed the anecdotes according to his own negative sensitivity to things European. Prutkov's creators were more interested in using certain foreign names and locales with a Prutkovian arbitrary purposefulness. A Russian love of things foreign may be ridiculed thereby, but, more importantly, the purely comic potential in such materials is wrung from them. Some of the anecdotes resemble expanded aphorisms, and one even ends with a Prutkovian aphorism. As is usual in Prutkov's works, even trivia have a didactic purpose; here the trivia may include "enlightenment" from the West.

Great men like Rousseau, Descartes, and Voltaire are used, not as an example, but as protagonists in some meaningless tale. Chronology is ignored, as Rousseau converses with a twelfth-century French abbot. Usually the names mentioned have the ring of wealth and title but nothing more, and the exploits read like an eighteenth-century society column. Some names, apparently foreign but not illustrious, sound meaningful in Russian, like the English lord Kučerston "known to all", the name suggesting a coachman in Russian. Sometimes the personages are anonymous, such as the engineer from the vicinity of Innsbruck or the "clever fourteenth-century scholar", given special attention at the court of the German Emperor. Usually, however, the anecdotes tend to illustrate the title of one of them, namely that "great people too are sometimes slow-witted".

The historical materials usually rely on the glitter of a name or title to get off a ridiculous story. In this they resemble the comedy *Blondy*. Prutkov was always obsessed with the glamour of the highly placed and the foreign; to this is added the glamour of the historical and the historical language in which historical happenings are described. Aside from these factors, the anecdotes betray another important Prutkovian trademark: they frequently involve excesses of behavior. One Prutkovian excess, stubbornness, resembles a Bergsonian mechanical action. In one story a minister remains faithful to his opinion when proved wrong.

---

[21] V. S. Solov'ev, "Prutkov K. P.", *Enciklopedičeskij slovar'* (Petersburg: Brokgauz-Efron, 1898), XXV, 634.
[22] F. M. Dostoevskij, *Sobranie sočinenij* (Moscow, 1956), IV, 75.

Kučerston has an accident with his carriage, hitting his head on the ground, and in order to show each guest how it happened, repeats it until he was deprived of his brain (presuming he had one to be deprived of). Ivan-Jakov de *(sic)* Rousseau waited for the twelfth-century abbot by a column for three days, until, "it is said", he starved to death. In Prutkov's poetry, his knights and barons often exhibit such self-defeating stubbornness.

A few of the anecdotes take the form of riddles, questions asked for no reason at all, and answered firmly but not quite to the point. Occasionally one senses the impatience of a Father William in the answers. Descartes, for instance, quite loses his temper when addressed.

Any anecdote, no matter how trivial, becomes grist for the Prutkovian mill: Prutkovian non-conclusions are drawn from non-premises. His authority is always imposed upon his reader, even in his smaller works. In his larger work, the *Project*, Prutkovian authority has a concrete social counterpart in the authority of Russian officialdom.

Vladimir Žemčužnikov reached the height of his purely satiric art in *Project: On introducing unity of thought in Russia (Proekt: o vvedenii edinomyslija v Rossii)*. This *Project* was published as part of the "Short Necrology and two posthumous works of K. P. Prutkov" in *Sovremennik* in 1863, but was prudently excluded from the *Complete Works* by Vladimir and republished only in 1932.[23]

Even when included in the body of Koz'ma Prutkov's works, it stands somewhat apart; the biting irony of its tone and its official form are quite unique. It is divided into an "attack" ("Pristup"), treatise ("traktat"), and conclusion ("zaključenie"). The "attack" takes the form of a sketchy, excited dialogue of Koz'ma Prutkov with himself. It asks the question: "Can people not honored with the confidence of the authorities really have an opinion of their own?" ("Da razve možet byt' sobstvennoe mnenie u ljudej, ne udostoennyx doveriem načal'stva?") Even writers, if they knew anything, would be called to government service. Prutkov prides himself on being the first to shake the authority of writers and makes a note to himself to develop this point. Žemčužnikov has retraced the steps of the bureaucratic mind which lead to censorship as if the latter did not yet exist. The irony is, of course, that it does exist.

Prutkov next proceeds to the treatise organized more formally in a series of questions and answers. Differences of opinion are the chief harm, he affirms. " 'A kingdom divided against itself' etc.", says Prutkov,

---

[23] *Literaturnoe nasledstvo* (1932), III, 197 ff.

either relying on the greater authority of the unfinished quotation or perhaps not knowing how to finish it. A series of illogical steps follows from the dubious premise, relying heavily on the accoutrements of logic and certainty of rhetoric. The great Russian nobleman does not wish to be mistaken. Where should he seek an opinion? From the authorities, of course. Having concluded this, Prutkov asks the loaded question:

> But how to know the opinion of the authorities? They tell us: it is evident from the measures taken. This is true. .... Hm! no! It is false! ... The government often keeps hidden its goals for higher considerations of state inaccessible to the understanding of the majority.

Prutkov has dug himself a hole and gets out of it, to his satisfaction alone, by saying that although government measures seem confused and contradictory, they are all part of a "single state plan; and that plan would stagger the mind with its immensity and with its consequences!" One must wait for history to unfold for it to be revealed. Here Prutkov quotes one of his own aphorisms about judging the whole, not the parts. Thus, the possibility of understanding without the grace of government is *nil*, but since the government is inscrutable and sheds its grace *ex post facto*, all understanding is impossible. The treatise concludes that the situation of people who seek the proper, official opinion is intolerable. Prutkov thereby destroys the whole logical edifice he has erected more quickly than could the most skillful opponent. Yet, sustained largely by the loftiness of his own words (he parenthetically praises a certain expression he has used), he proceeds to the conclusion.

The conclusion covers over half the text. In seventy-eight words, its first sentence summarizes the problem stated in the treatise and proposes its solution in the creation of a government publication to give "governing views on every matter". Thus there would be no need for questions. Prutkov rhetorically asks: "For what do they lead to?" and emphatically states, "the true patriot must be the enemy of all so-called 'questions'!" At the point where the *Project* has begun to sound all too familiar, the purely Prutkovian takes over and pure humor relieves the tensions which satire has built up. Prutkov affirms that the choice of an editor of such a government organ is the crucial matter and, while his modesty prevents him from proposing himself for the job, he does so anyway. He cites as a qualification his long experience in government finances, which need official explanations as badly as anything else.

The chief charm of the *Project* lies in its somewhat breathless tone. Prutkov is proposing a huge government organization which would completely control all opinion and thought, a scheme frightening in its already partially realized potential. But his style, full of contradictions, belies the inevitable "logic" of his thesis. His long participial phrases and sequential format are continually undercut by breathless excitement at having found the apt turn of phrase and by the final triumphant entry of his own person. He surmounts his argument and, beaming with pride, sits on it.

Prutkov appears at his most ominous in the *Project*. The idea that in some situations a person with Prutkovian limitations presumes to advise, instruct, and command could have serious as well as comic possibilities. One does not think of such possibilities in the poetry. The poems, with their extremely skillful clumsiness, seem to have their own reason for being. They speak directly to the reader only in standard poetic forms of address. In the prose, however, Koz'ma Prutkov occasionally seems to speak to the reader with the proximity and familiarity of oral speech; at times, although not a sustained narrative, approximating a form of *skaz*.[24] B. Ja. Buxštab contrasted Koz'ma Prutkov as *skaz* with Koz'ma Prutkov as *mistifikacija*:

> The criteria of success of mystifications lies, of course, in the extent to which they are believed by the readers, who do not guess that they are being hoaxed. But here is a more complicated phenomenon; here is a *skaz* ... by a tale-telling persona, a parodied grotesque hero. If the authors wanted the reader to believe seriously in the existence of Koz'ma Prutkov, they would, of course, not have attributed their parodies to him, but maybe such a dullard as Koz'ma Prutkov could not have written even one of such works as his tutors gave him. According to the task of the author, the reader should at once feel both the monolithic wholeness and the complete illusoriness of the "author-personality" of Koz'ma Prutkov; otherwise he cannot be a parodied hero.[25]

Koz'ma Prutkov undoubtedly began as a sort of mystification, for the readers did not know who he was. But the question of believing seriously in his existence is not as essential as that of seriously believing in the importance of his fictional existence. As a sort of *skaz* (even though his voice changes when chronology—i.e., whether he is writing as an eighteenth or nineteenth century man—or censorship requires) Prutkov's

---

[24] The best and most concise definition of *skaz* is the following: "It means a stylistically individualized inner narrative placed in the mouth of a fictional character and designed to produce the illusion of oral speech." Hugh McLean, "On the Style of a Leskovian Skaz", *Harvard Slavic Studies* (1954), II, 299.

[25] B. Ja. Buxštab, "Estetizm v poezii 40-60-x gg. i parodii Koz'my Prutkova", *Trudy otdela novoj russkoj literatury* (Moscow–Leningrad: A. N. Institut russkoj literatury, 1948), I, 172.

prose forms a coherent block. In his poetry, however, as we shall see in the following chapter, the personality of Prutkov seems chameleon-like; it takes on the coloration of the different poetic schools he imitates. In addition, the cleverness of the poems tempts one to forget the illusion of the not so clever fictional author. Still, Prutkov never quite lets the reader forget when he is writing poetry that he is *being a poet*. His poetic vocation is pursued as consciously as his prosaic, bureaucratic one.

Prutkov is, therefore, a blatantly fictional being writing works that are undeniably real (we not only hear about them; we read them) and which in turn make his fictional existence important. Prutkov, lacking wit, pays homage to himself in his works and his works wittily return the compliment. Thus, in the largest sense, Koz'ma Prutkov is a parody of the relationship, partly premeditated and ultimately fortuitous, between an author and his work.

The prose and the poetry are meant to combine into a whole, but they really have more of a mutually additive relationship. Prutkov's guardians wished to have it both ways: they wanted the imposing personality of the bureaucrat Prutkov as he appears in his prose, and they wanted the artistic brilliance of the poetry. The two may at times be inconsistent, but the reader has little grounds for complaint when two separate delights fail to correspond consistently.

V

THE POETRY:
PARODY IN THEORY AND IN PRACTICE

When he wrote poetry, Koz'ma Prutkov used many of the traditional poetic genres—including the fable, the epigram, the album verse, the short lyric, the romance, and the ballad. His use of genre is parodic. By the mid-nineteenth century the use of a specific genre no longer necessarily entailed a certain level of diction or a particular metrical and rhyme pattern. The first thing to go had been the hierarchy of genre, although even in the eighteenth century every genre was judged by its own standards within the hierarchy. As Voltaire had said and Batjuškov had reiterated, "all genres are good except the boring..."[1] The great poets of the 1820's and 1830's used genres like the elegy, each in his own way. Nevertheless, most poets still thought in terms of previously set genres, and some identified themselves with a certain genre which they used repeatedly. New genres appeared and old ones continued to be modified, but rather than dictating the form, the genre often found itself reduced to a mere subtitle, a suggestion of a tradition. Often it indicated only the fervent wish of a minor poet to follow his more illustrious predecessors or to capitalize on some newly-acquired trend from the West, like the romance. Prutkov would want to prove his versatility by writing as many kinds of poetry as all his contemporaries put together. He would then (to use Tynjanov's image) reach into the cupboard and find ready-made the genre he needed.[2] In addition, Prutkov's creators gained a distinct advantage in the art of humor by the parodic use of genre. By using essentially "rational" and predetermined modes of style, they could give free rein to irrational and unpredicatable notions. By setting limits, they could reach beyond them.

[1] K. N. Batjuškov, *Sočinenija* (Moscow, 1955), p. 382.
[2] Ju. N. Tynjanov, "Promežutok", *Arxaisty i novatory* (Leningrad: Priboj, 1929), p. 574.

No one element determines the humor of a particular Prutkovian genre. In any individual work, however, one element of humor may predominate—the sound of a word, a single figure such as that of the romantic poet, or a single comic situation involving many characters.

The element of parody, the distance between the fanciful creation of Prutkov and some real work by a real poet, also varies greatly: some poems appear clearly as parodies of a single work, some are vague parodies of a literary tendency, some contain pure humor and little or no parody. Most critics of Prutkov find two main currents in his work—one of parody and one of alogism. They then venture upon a demonstration of which stream dominates the other.[3] Most often, however, it is extremely difficult to separate such "currents" even in a single work, let alone to measure their relative importance. As with most other literary variables, even if parodic and alogic devices could be counted, frequency alone would not determine importance. Also, the relation between parody and alogic has great intricacy, like the proverbial chicken and the egg. Usually the creators of Koz'ma Prutkov seized upon what was illogical (to them) in a work and parodied it by exaggerating it or by shifting this one element into a whole new context. But often this very element is hard to discern in its new setting, after it has suffered a Prutkovian change, so that the whole work appears purely humorous. When, as we have seen, Vladimir Žemčužnikov carefully preserved or added a subtitle dedicating the poem to Benediktov, Fet, or Grigor'ev, he was anxious for his readers to "get the joke", for in 1884 readers would not be able to detect much of the parody in Prutkov's works. Žemčužnikov was right in seizing upon the parodic element as an additional source of humor, but the fact that Prutkov's works are appreciated today with little or no reference to any other works shows that their humor is far from dependent upon parody alone.

---

[3]   P. K. Guber opts for alogic, P. N. Berkov sees a more or less equal division between parody and alogic, and A. A. Morozov and I. A. Sukiasova say that nearly all the works of Prutkov can be considered parody of some sort. See: Koz'ma Prutkov, *Proizvedenija ne vošedšie v sobranie sočinenij*, ed. P. K. Guber, p. 18; P. N. Berkov, *Koz'ma Prutkov, direktor Probirnoj palatki i poet (K istorii russkoj parodii)*, passim; A. A. Morozov, "Parodija kak literaturnyj žanr (k teorii parodii)", *Russkaja literatura* (1960), No. 1, p. 60; and I. M. Sukiasova, *Jazyk i stil' parodij Koz'my Prutkova*, p. 85. D. Čiževskij, in a general discussion of parody, makes the same division in different terms. He distinguishes "literary parody" from "comic parody" or "naughty verse" ("ozornoe stixotvorenie"), but he does not really test these classifications in grey areas. See Dmitrij Čiževskij, "O literaturnoj parodii", *Novyj žurnal*, No. 79 (June, 1965), pp. 121-140.

Vladimir Žemčužnikov, while organizing the *Complete Works*, grouped Koz'ma Prutkov's efforts into fables, stage works, prose, and verse.[4] The fables of Prutkov form a distinct and large unit. There are thirteen of them, and all but one ("Pjatki nekstati", written by Vladimir himself) were included in the *Complete Works*. Fables, as we have seen, were among the earliest of Prutkov's works, and led directly to the invention of Prutkov himself. The first ones were written in 1851 and most of the others before the end of 1855. All three Žemčužnikovs, Tolstoj, and two "outsiders", Ammosov and Eršov, had a hand in their creation.

The shortest fable, "The Cowherd, the Milk, and the Reader" ("Pastux, moloko, i čitatel' ") was written by A. N. Ammosov:[5]

> Однажды нес пастух куда-то молоко.
>   Но так ужасно далеко,
>   Что уж назад не возвращался.
> Читатель! он тебе не попадался?

> Once a cowherd took some milk,
>   But he went so far astray,
>   That he never did return.
> Reader! has he passed your way?

It substitutes a question for a moral and manages to pack the three "protagonists" of the title into a four-line plot. P. P. Eršov wrote the epigram which inspired Prutkov's "Epigramma No. II" (also known as "Oprometčivost' "). Vladimir Žemčužnikov vastly improved the epigram from an unpublished cycle by Eršov by enriching the pun.[6]

Most of Prutkov's fables follow the standard pattern. Their language is colloquial, artfully simple and free of figures of speech, for fables themselves are a kind of metaphor. They often (but not always) involve animals, but really concern human deeds and social relations. The professional "inside dopester"-Zagoreckij in Griboedov's *Woe from Wit*

---

[4] See the letter of February 18 to A. N. Pypin: Koz'ma Prutkov, pp. 397-98.
[5] This fact is indicated in two letters. *Ibid.*, p. 437. Ammosov (1823-66) also wrote other works under the pseudonym "Posledovatel' Kuz'my Prutkova".
[6] B. Ja. Buxštab, "Koz'ma Prutkov, P. P. Eršov i N. A. Cižov", *Omskij almanax*, V (1945), 129. The Prutkovian epigram runs:

> Раз архитектор с птичницей спознался.
> И что ж? — в их детище смешались две натуры:
> Сын архитектора, он строить покушался;
> Потомок птичницы, он строил только — куры.

(III, 21) perceived this double meaning and declared that if he were the censor, he would "crack down on fables", for the lions and eagles in them are really Tsars. The fable consists of an introduction, usually some dialogue, and a concluding moral. Prutkovian fables have one essential difference. Ordinary fables generally satirize some aspect of society and point a moral relevant to the situation described. Koz'ma Prutkov's fables have no internal logic and their moral is irrelevant or unconnected to their story; thus it becomes impossible for them to make any satiric point.

Some critics, therefore, have regarded them as parody. It is true that the golden age of the Russian fable was past. It had begun in the seventeenth century with Simeon Polockij, was developed in the eighteenth century by Trediakovskij, Kantemir, Sumarokov, Xemnicer, Izmailov and Dmitriev, and reached its apogee with Krylov. Throughout the whole of the nineteenth century the difficult art of the fable was declining. Koz'ma Prutkov was ahead of the satirists of the sixties in attempting to write fables, but he had several minor predecessors of a different sort in the forties. Among them were B. M. Fedorov, whom Prutkov mentions in the first variant to his "Project" as a worthly colleague.[7] K. Masal'skij's fables appeared at the beginning of 1851 (the first Prutkovian fables were written that summer) and called forth mocking reviews in *Moskvitjanin* and most other journals.[8] In the trite fables of the day, the moral was weak and the story often not to the point. Still, no specific parallels can be made between Prutkov's fables and these; rather, Prutkovian fables imitate the really good ones of Aesop, La Fontaine and Krylov in their scheme. With Prutkov, as one theorist wrote of successful fables in general "the fable falls into two moments; the development destroys the line traced out in the initial situation, adding to it an unexpected contradictory result."[9] Prutkov has taken the essence of the good fable, its quality of surprise, and called attention to it by exaggeration.

Perhaps the first Prutkovian fable written was "Nezabudki i zapjatki" ("Forget-me-nots and Footboards"—the alliterative pun of "ne*zabudki*-

---

[7] Koz'ma Prutkov, ed. P. N. Berkov, p. 384.
[8] Berkov, p. 63. See Sukiasova, pp. 85-86, for examples of weak fables.
[9] Lidija Vindt, "Basnja kak literaturnyj žanr", *Poetika* (Leningrad: Academia, 1927), III, 88. When Puškin and Jazykov attempted a joint parody of Dmitriev's fables [see Dmitrij Tschiževskij, ed., *Russische literarische Parodien* (Wiesbaden: Otto Harrassowitz, 1957), p. 19, for example], they exaggerated the dullness, neglected the quality of surprise, and the result is far below Prutkov.

zapjatki" is lost in translation, but in the Russian it establishes an even greater connection than the conjunction "i" between the two words, obviously far removed in shape, texture, smell, color, and just about everything else). The fable is divided into the usual narrative and concluding moral:

> Трясясь Пахомыч на запятках,
> Пук незабудок вез с собой;
> Мозоли натерев на пятках,
> Лечил их дома камфарой.

> Читатель! в басне сей откинув незабудки,
> Здесь помещенные для шутки,
> Ты только это заключи:
> Коль будут у тебя мозоли,
> То, чтоб избавиться от боли,
> Ты, как Пахомыч наш, их камфарой лечи.

> Paxomyč bumping on the wheels,
> Took some forget-me-nots along;
> Acquiring bunions on his heels,
> He treated them with camphor strong.

> Pray, drop the flowers of which we spoke,
> They're only added for a joke,
> This problem has one answer:
> If your bunions hurt again,
> In order to relieve the pain,
> Like our Paxomyč, pamper them with camphor.

The reader wonders what the forget-me-nots will do in the story, and he is told (literally and figuratively) to drop them. Instead, he receives some down-to-earth advice about treating bunions. The flowers are a joke; bunions are serious. The diction, rhymes and puns are all most playful. The word "puk" has humorous associations (it recalls the word *pukat'* 'to fart'). The forget-me-nots are admittedly put in for a joke, and the heels *(pjatki)* are obviously there because they rhyme with footboards *(zapjatki)*. This echo-rhyme, which Tynjanov would call a punning rhyme *(kalamburnaja rifma)*[10] relies on an exaggerated accuracy. The other rhymes in this fable, and in all Prutkov's fables, adhere to a strict scheme. The one followed here is ababccdeed. Some of the longer fables, for

---

[10]   Ju. N. Tynjanov, *Problema stixotvornogo jazyka* (Leningrad, 1924), p. 114.

instance "The Landlord and the Gardener" ("Pomeščik i sadovnik")
have an even more rigid rhyme pattern. Clearly the rhyme play itself is
the most important element of a good fable. Like the story of the fable,
it tantalizes the reader with an anticipatory suspense and its fulfillment
always provides something of a surprise. It hovers between the accidental
and the inevitable.

Whether enthusiastic for or mystified by his fables, Prutkov's contemporaries seemed not to perceive them as parody. Upon their first publication in *Sovremennik*, A. V. Družinin waxed so enthusiastic over "The
Driver and the Tarantula" ("Konduktor i tarantul") that he devoted
several paragraphs to embroidering upon it, making that short joke into
a long one. His praise is tongue-in-cheek, but he seems to treat the fable
as pure humor rather than as parody.[11] When the *Complete Works*
came out, several critics merely found the fables infuriating. One objects
to their lack of "moral teaching or in general any idea at all".[12] Another
critic dislikes the fable "The Landlord and the Gardener" because it
shows no trace of parody:

In it we have no allusion to any reality, there is nothing comic or even witty:
this is simply a rather absurd joke ... a most guileless and hardly witty play
on words, with no further significance. We meet such verses of Koz'ma Prutkov
often, with even more "obscure" meaning, with even more "perplexing" aims.
In others of his "experiments" Koz'ma Prutkov more successfully parodies
this or that poetic genre, this or that poet—and in essence the significance of
Koz'ma Prutkov is to be found precisely in parody, at times very successful and
sharp.[13]

Other readers who prefer parody (the more satiric the better) to simple
light verse would find Prutkov's fables the weaker part of his work. Some
are not without satirical overtones, but often they consist of a pun and
nothing more.

A. A. Morozov claims that "parody of a genre is not necessarily tied
to style", although "parody of a genre nearly always includes a parody
of the style of a concrete author". He asks: "What parodied stylistic level
stands behind the fables of Prutkov, although their parodic quality
(parodijnost') doubtless exists?"[14] Morozov's theory is debatable. Parody

[11] A. V. Družinin, *Polnoe sobranie sočinenij* (Petersburg, 1865), VI, 559-63.
[12] Anon., "Polnoe sobranie sočinenij K. Prutkova", *Delo*, N. 3 (1884), p. 53.
[13] V. V. Cujko, "Jumoristy", *Sovremennaja russkaja poezija v ee predstaviteljax*
(Petersburg, 1885), p. 178.
[14] Morozov, pp. 55-56.

implies stylistic imitation, whether it be of a specific author or of a specific genre. If a genre is used by an author to write humorous poetry, it does not necessarily mean that the author is parodying the genre itself. Numerous poets have found themes and forms from nursery rhymes convenient points of departure for humorous verse, relying on the factor of recognition by the reader in order to surprise him with a new element; yet these poems could not strictly be labelled parodies on nursery rhymes. There is a point, and Prutkov's fables reach it, at which parody of a genre fades into light verse written in that genre.

The ordinary fable is both humorous and didactic; Prutkov's fables are only the former, unless their moral be that the idea of a moral is in itself humorous, because it is superfluous. Sometimes Prutkov's fables merely pun, sometimes they give conservative or self-evident advice, and, at their best, they approach a perfection either of pseudo-satire or of pure absurdity.

The least successful of the fables involve puns and nothing more. The critic who expressed annoyance at "The Landlord and the Gardener" complained justifiably. It is nothing but a pun based on multiple meanings of the word "prozjabat' "—to vegetate and to freeze. The fable "Figure and Voice" ("Stan i golos") is based on a richer kind of pun: one formed by homonyms.[15] In it a district police-officer (stanovoj) envies aloud the voice of a turtle-dove. If he had such a voice, he could sing beautiful songs to his mother-in-law. But the wise turtle-dove replies: "And I envy you your fate: to me has been given a voice, to you a figure (*stan*, which also means a district police bureau). The line runs: "A ja tvoej zaviduju sud'be:/Mne golos dan, a stan tebe." In this rather simple fable there is delight to be had in hearing a whole tale woven out of a mere pun. The previously mentioned fable called "Epigramma No. II" or "Oprometčivost' " takes the form of a four-line epigram and is based on a triple pun, thanks to the help of Frenchified Russian. The offspring of an architect and a poultry maid had two natures: "on stroil ... kury"—meaning both: he built courts and, in French-Russian, he paid court *(stroit' kury* means *faire la cour)*. *Kury* in plain Russian, however, means chickens.

In three of the fables puns are used with satiric effect. In "The Landlord and the Grass" ("Pomeščik i trava") a landlord's would-be generosity is foiled by his agricultural ignorance. In "The Bureaucrat and the Chicken" ("Činovnik i kurica") the two protagonists are united to con-

---

[15] For distinctions between various forms of puns in Russian, see: A. A. Sčerbina, *Suščnost' i iskusstvo ostroty (kalambura)*, (Kiev, 1958).

trast the frantic but pointless activity of the man with the peaceful pro-
ductivity of the bird. In "The Star and th e Belly" ("Zvezda i brjuxo"),
the empty belly synecdochically represents its fasting owner and the
moral is to become a general so as not to be obliged to fast. These fables
are less successful, for in all three the pun is too long in coming. Even
when taken as purposeful humorlessness, the fable's punning and the
satire work against each other. P. I. Vejnberg caught this contradiction
and wrote the only parody on Prutkov: his fable "Trostnik i spina"
successfully parodies "Zvezda i brjuxo".[16]

One of the best satiric fables involves no pun at all. It was written by
Vladimir Žemčužnikov, who did well to change its title from "A Lesson
to Grandsons" ("Urok vnučatam"), as it had appeared in *Sovremennik*,
to "A Difference of Tastes" ("Raznica vkusov") in the *Complete Works*.
The fable in effect reduces all differences to a question of taste. At dinner
one night there occurs a conflict between age and youth about a literal
difference in taste, the taste of food. The irate grandfather tells his grandson, "To you bitter horseradish is like raspberry,/But to me blanc-mange
is wormwood." What seems an essential truth—that life is sweet to the
young and bitter to the old—is not the point at all, as we see from the
conclusion which tells the reader that "we differ in fate and all the more
in taste" (emphasizing the less essential of the two) and that "you rave
about Berlin;/I prefer Medyn'." (A provincial Russian town in Kaluga
province). The proverbial "chacun à son goût" has been exploded by
stuffing too many things into it. The fable itself is ambiguous: is it
mocking differences between men, reducing them to a matter of taste,
or does it satirize the peacemaker who ignores vital differences by doing
so? The copy of the *Complete Works* of 1884 prepared for the new 1885
edition[17] contains some notes by Vladimir Žemčužnikov which provide
a clue. They tell an anecdote similar to this one, except that the protagonists are a Westernizer and a Slavophile. The latter would naturally
prefer a Russian hick-town to a foreign capital and center of learning
where many Westernizing Russians studied. Koz'ma Prutkov, his patriotism aroused, sides with the Slavophile. In the text as it was actually
printed, a footnote states only that this was a true incident in the family
of Koz'ma Prutkov; thus the satiric reference is only hinted at. Apparently
Vladimir Žemčužnikov felt in this instance that obvious satire lay outside
Prutkov's peculiar province.

[16]   A. Amfiteatrov, ed., *Zabytyj smex* (Moscow, 1917), II, 51.
[17]   Institut russkoj literatury (Puškinskij dom), ANSSSR, Rukopisnyj otdel.

Prutkov's real talent as a fabulist lay in the realm of the absurd.
The fable entitled "Heels Inappropriate" ("Pjatki nekstati") is as removed
from logic as a Limerick by Lear:

У кого болит затылок,
Тот уж пяток не чеши!
Мой сосед был слишком пылок
(Жил в деревне он, в глуши):
Раз случись ему, гуляя,
Головой задеть сучок:
Он, недолго размышляя,
Осердяся на толчок,
Хвать рукой за обе пятки —
И затем в грязь носом хвать!

Многие привычки гадки,
Но скверней не отыскать
Пятки попусту чесать!

If it itches on your head,
Don't begin to scratch your heels!
My neighbor was by passion led.
(He lived in country, in the fields):
Once this man, as he went walking,
Brushed his head against a tree;
Considered it and hardly balking,
Took the bump quite angrily,
Grabbed both heels and with a thud
Took a nose-dive in the mud.

There are many vicious habits,
But no nastier may be sought
Than to scratch one's heels for nought.

It begins with a moral and ends with a stern commentary. The whimsical
behavior of the country gentleman is described in rational, even meter
and neat cross rhymes, but there is no logical connection between lines
three and four or lines eight and nine. The author, Vladimir Žemčužnikov, too modestly decided not to include this fable in the *Complete
Works*, but its whimsey suits modern tastes perfectly. Finally, "The
Driver and the Tarantula", the fable Družinin singled out, has a beautiful
structure to support its absurdity.

В горах Гишпании тяжелый экипаж
С кондуктором отправился в вояж.

Гишпанка, севши в нем, немедленно заснула.
　　А муж ее меж тем, увидя тарантул́а,
　　　　Вскричал: «Кондуктор, стой!
　　　　Приди скорей! Ах, боже мой!»
　　На крик кондуктор поспешает
И тут же веником скотину выгоняет,
Примолвив: «Денег ты за место не платил!»
И тотчас же его пят́ою раздавил.

Читатель! разочти вперед свои депансы,
Чтоб даром не дерзать садиться в дилижансы,
　　　　И норови, чтобы отнюдь
　　　　Без денег не пускаться в путь;
Не то случится и с тобой, что с насекомым,
　　　　　　Тебе знакомым.

In the Spanish mountains a heavy equipage
　　　　With its driver set out en voyage.
A Spanish lady slept inside. Her
Husband, meanwhile, glimpsed a giant spider
　　　　And cried, "Oh driver, wait!
　　　　Come quickly; it may be too late!"
　　　　The driver hurried at the shout
And with a broom swept the beast out.
He said, "You haven't bought a ticket!"
And with his heel began to kick it.

Friend! Calculate ahead all your expenses,
Do not sit down in vain in diligences,
　　　　But follow, please, this precedent:
　　　　Do not set forth without a cent,
Unless you seek the fate of that same pet
　　　　Whom you have met.

The first two lines conjure up an exotic landscape, but the Spanish
mountains and the Spanish lady have nothing to do with the plot. Still,
the story seems rational until the driver begins to speak to the tarantula
(a more sonorous word in Russian than in English), who then serves as
an example for the reader. The last two lines, long and short, seem to
echo the rational development and irrational dénouement of the whole
fable.

It has been noted in connection with the biographies of Prutkov's creators
that Prutkov's verse seems to grow out of society and occasional verse
more than out of any standard humorous or satirical genre. The fables

are close relatives of really polished *vers de société*. As one critic defined it:

> Genuine *vers de société* and *vers d'occasion* should be short, elegant, refined, and fanciful, not seldom distinguished by chastened sentiment, and often playful. The tone should not be pitched high; it should be idiomatic and rather in the conversational key; the rhythm should be crisp and sparkling, and the rhyme frequent and never forced, while the entire poem should be marked by tasteful moderation, high finish, and completeness; for, however trivial the subject-matter may be, indeed rather in proportion to its triviality, subordination to the rules of composition and perfection of execution should be strictly enforced.[18]

If Koz'ma Prutkov created works of monumental triviality, credit must go to his "guardians" for the perfection of their execution.

The epigram and the album verse, two of the most common forms taken in occasional verse, appear more than once in Prutkov's works. He would naturally wish to exercise an impromptu wit by writing them. The three epigrams Prutkov wrote are all quite devoid of wit, but full of technical sparkle—sound puns, alliteration, deliberate sequences of tautologies and non sequiturs. If they are written to or against someone, the unfortunate addressee is not mentioned by name. The shortest epigrams written in strict alexandrines, has but two lines:

> «Вы любите ли сыр?» — спросили раз ханжу.
> «Люблю, — он отвечал, — я вкус в нем нахожу».

> "And are you fond of cheese?"—they asked the bigot once.
> "I am—he answered them,—"It's rather nice to munch."

The rhyme *xan-žu*/*nax-a-žu* is quite clever and it is enlightening to learn that one can be a bigot even about cheese. Next, consider the triple tautology backed by alliteration in another epigram:

> Мне, в размышлении глубоком,
> Сказал однажды Лизимах:
> «Что зрячий зрит здоровым оком,
> Слепой не видит и в очках!»

> In profoundest meditation,
> Lysimachus said one time:
> "Seers see with healthy vision,
> The blind with glasses still are blind."

[18] Friedrich Locker-Lampson, ed., *Lyra Elegantiarum* (New York: F. A. Stokes and Brother, 1889), p. vii.

Prutkov enjoyed using classical references in his epigrams, in what was really classical name-dropping. Lysimachus, one of Alexander's generals, is somewhat removed in time from Prutkov. His Greeks are often mentioned illogically as well as unchronologically. In the third epigram, Prutkov also proves that two non sequitors are better than one:

> Пия душистый сок цветочка,
> Пчела дает нам мед взамен;
> Хотя твой лоб пустая бочка,
> Но всё же ты не Диоген.

> Drinking the fragrant flower's their task,
> We get our honey from the bees;
> Although your head's an empty cask
> You still are no Diogenes.

The verses which filled the albums of young ladies in Petersburg and Moscow salons in the first half of the nineteenth century were written by everyone from the Puškins to the Lenskijs, paying compliments sometimes ironic and sometimes sincere. We have already seen how the joking verse by Aleksej Žemčužnikov "In the Album of N. N." mocked the very metaphor it created and, more generally, mocked poetry that favored the proliferation of serpents of melancholy. The other album verse, "In the Album of a Beautiful Foreigner" ("V al'bom krasivoj čužestranke"), was written by Vladimir Žemčužnikov. It parodies a poem of A. S. Xomjakov "To a Foreign Woman" ("Inostranke") written in 1831 and included in Xomjakov's 1844 collection "25 Verses"—a poem whose exaggerated content fairly cried out for parody even more than twenty years later. In Xomjakov's poem the poet refuses to give his love to the beautiful foreigner upon whom his ecstatic gaze is fixed, for her heart does not tremble when he whispers "Holy Rus' " to her. (She does not understand Russian.) Žemčužnikov merely shortened the poem from twenty-eight lines to eight, divided neatly into four of praise and four of reservations, made the language more colloquial, and changed the pronouns of the person addressed from Xomjakov's third person to a familar second person:

> Вокруг тебя очарованье.
> Ты бесподобна. Ты мила.
> Ты силой чудной обаянья
> К себе поэта привлекла.

Но он любить тебя не можеть:
Ты родилась в чужом краю,
И он охулки не положит,
Любя тебя, на честь свою.

Around you an enchanted bower.
You are unequalled. You are sweet.
By wondrous fascinating power
You've brought the poet to your feet.
But from your love he must refrain:
For you were born abroad somewhere,
And he's no dope to go and stain,
By loving you, his honor fair.

This xenophobic ditty was not Prutkov's only poetic tribute to the Slavophiles, as we shall see.

The greater part of Prutkov's short verse is marked by what can best be termed extravagance. The Žemčužnikovs and Tolstoj were quick to detect the exaggerated in any genre, in any school of poetry, in the works of any one poet, or in any one particular work. They saw it in poetic poses, romantic and neo-classical, in the fixed ideas and structural repetitions of the epic, and in the styles which embellished philosophical extravagance or which extravagantly camouflaged a lack of substance. Whether speaking as a bureaucrat or as a poet, Prutkov exaggerated the language of the two and sometimes even mixed them, for he was a romantic bureaucrat and a pedantic poet. He insisted upon certain words and poses until they became Prutkovian trademarks.

Beneath the variety of poems and poets parodied and the even greater variety of Prutkov's poetic output, there lie certain constants. All the poetry parodied by Prutkov had a personal, "romantic" tinge to it; all the parodies of Prutkov isolate certain features of this romanticism, exaggerate it and contrast it to a more "realistic" view of life. Russian theorists of parody, beginning with Tynjanov, have postulated the reader's awareness of a "second level" as a prerequisite for parody. In the most recent formulation by A. A. Morozov, the contrastive effect of parody is stressed:

In order for parody to arise, there must be a definite relation to the "second level"—skeptical, ironic, friendly, mocking, joking, or sarcastic—one or another, but decidedly contrasting with the original, breaking, displacing, and often destroying the habitual perception.[19]

[19] Morozov, p. 51.

In a work of parody this contrast is usually implicit. The voice of the parodist and the imitative voice he adopts for his parodic purpose merge. However, in one of Prutkov's most famous poems, the contrast between the folly of the one and the reason of the other is made explicit in the two opposing quatrains:

> Вянет лист. Проходит лето.
>   Иней серебрится. . .
> Юнкер Шмидт из пистолета
>   Хочет застрелиться.
>
> Погоди, безумный, снова
>   Зелень оживится!
> Юнкер Шмидт! честно́е слово,
>   Лето возвратится!

> Fades the leaf. The summer's over.
>   Hoar-frost starts to fall.
> Junker Schmidt with a revolver
>   Wants to end it all.
>
> Wait, oh madman, somewhere yonder
>   Green you will discern!
> Junker Schmidt, my word of honor,
>   Summer will return!

The second quatrain breaks in with the earnest appeal of logic. The only cause given for Junker Schmidt's incipient suicide is the passing of summer, so it is only natural to remind him that summer will return. Of course, the romantic metaphor ironically opposes the renewal of nature to the aging of man, but when this metaphor has been made concrete, despair is meaningless. Or perhaps, since romantic heroes despair while they are still young, Prutkov has perfect "reason" to chide them. The accent on čestnóe heightens its absurdity by giving it ecclesiastical connotations and further contributes to the clumsy earnestness of the poem.

"Junker Schmidt" is ultimately the parody of a pose, not of a metaphor, and probably it parodies a specific poem. Its very simplicity has tempted critics to find its source of inspiration. The author, Aleksej Tolstoj, often refers to Junker Schmidt in his letters, and he has become the archtypal Prutkovian romantic hero, but no one knows his exact predecessor. "Junker Schmidt" was first printed under the title "From Heine", and in the 1884 edition Vladimir Žemčužnikov subtitled it "Perhaps—from Heine". Most critics have searched in vain for Heine's corresponding verse,[20] and concluded that the poem would not have been typical of Heine, but more probably of his Russian imitators. Berkov suggests a similarity to a poem by E. Rostopčina,[21] but Buxštab has abandoned all specific comparison. The poem has a strong, heretofore unnoticed resemblance to a quatrain in a poem by Karamzin called "Osen' ", written in 1789.

> Странник печальный, утешься!
> > Вянет Природа
> Только на малое время;
> > Всё оживится,

> Wanderer forlorn, take comfort!
> > Nature fades
> Only for a short time;
> > Everything will come alive.

Nevertheless, the delicate irony of Heine's own verse should not be discounted as a direct inspiration for Prutkov, especially when there exists a poem of his as close to "Junker Šmidt" as this one:[22]

> Das Fräulein stand am Meere
> Und seufzte lang und bang,
> Es rührte sie so sehre
> Der Sonnenuntergang.

> "Mein Fraülein! sein Sie munter,
> Das ist ein altes Stück;
> Hier vorne geht sie unter
> Und kehrt von hinten zurück."

Good parody need not feed upon bad poetry alone, as any collection of parody over the years in any language will show us.[23] Presumably a skillful parodist, determined to get to the essence of a work and ridicule it by exaggeration, could seize upon anything that has ever been written. His parody can express admiration, as in the case of Prutkov and Heine, as well as mockery.

---

[20]   Čiževskij claims to have found the poem, but does not name it. Čiževskij, p. 137.
[21]   *Koz'ma Prutkov*, ed. Berkov, p. 533.
[22]   Heinrich Heine, *Werke und Briefe* (Berlin: Aufbau Verlag, 1961), I, 240.
[23]   See bibliography.

In general, Prutkovian parodies were not aimed primarily at separate authors, let alone separate poems, although the repeated themes of an author or the exaggerated verbiage of a given poem may have triggered a particular parody. The parody of Koz'ma Prutkov is directed against certain literary habits, certain outmoded and overblown literary fashions of a preceding age. They seem to take certain refrains and poses as a pretext for deflating an entire era, the age of romanticism. This era may be seen as stretching from the sentimentalist Karamzin and pre-romanticism of Žukovskij to the "classical" romanticism of Ščerbina, the verbally innovating romanticism of Benediktov, and the patriotic romanticism of the Slavophiles.

An argument for the connection between romanticism and nonsense parody would produce interesting facts of supranational literary history. Certainly nonsense enjoyed its greatest day in England in the wake of the romantic movement.[24] In Russia the nonsense tradition, small as it is, has fed upon romanticism in the nineteenth century and upon neo-romantic symbolism in the twentieth (for example, in the parodies of Solov'ev and Izmajlov).

Parody itself is non-"romantic". It looks with an exaggerated realism upon the emotional, philosophic or descriptive excesses of literature, or of a character such as Junker Schmidt. While a parody of a romantic work may be realistically prosaic, a parody of a realistic work will never be romantic, but will tend (as do the many parodies of Hemingway) to strip realism even barer. Prutkov's parody of romanticism thus could take a wide variety of forms, alternating between the wildly exaggerated and the sober, ranging freely over the lush, overgrown territory of an outgrown epoch.

The poem entitled "My Portrait" complements the engraved portrait of Prutkov and traditionally appears as the first poem in Prutkov's *Works*. It demonstrates with perfection of style what Prutkov did to the figure of the romantic poet, and the fact that Prutkov is a collaboration adds a further touch of unreality to this ultra-individual.

---

[24] This point has been made, but not developed, in Emile Cammaerts, *The Poetry of Nonsense* (New York: Dutton, 1926), p. 85. In Germany there are certain similarities between the humorous writings of Ludwig Eichrodt and Prutkov. Eichrodt used the character Biedermaier as one of several pseudonymns in his *Anthology of Lyrical Caricatures*, first published in 1850. Biedermaier, a retired schoolmaster, writes poetry. Like Prutkov, he praises law and authority and himself. He uses Goethe and Schiller much as Prutkov does the ancient Greeks—for purposes of lofty conversation. He too is a relic of the romantic age, of pre-1848 Germany. See: Ludwig Eichrodt, *Lyrische Karikaturen: eine Anthologie* (Lahr, 1869).

Когда в толпе ты встретишь человека,
Который наг;[25]
Чей лоб мрачней туманного Казбека,
Неровен шаг;
Кого власы подъяты в беспорядке;
Кто, вопия,
Всегда дрожит в нервическом припадке, —
Знай: это я!

Кого язвят, со злостью вечно новой,
Из рода в род;
С кого толпа венец его лавровый
Безумно рвет;
Кто ни пред кем спины не клонит гибкой, —
Знай: это я!. .
В моих устах спокойная улыбка,
В груди — змея!

When in the crowd you meet a man somehow,
Who naked goes;[26]
Gloomier than the fogged Kazbek his brow,
Unsure he roves;
Whose tresses rumple up in disarray;
Who, with a cry,
Forever trembles in a nervous way,—
Know: it is I!

Whom people taunt in ever-growing quarrel,
Throughout the years;
From whom the madding throng his wreath of laurel
In folly tears;
Who before no man bends his knee so supple,
Know: it is I!
Upon my lips there plays a smile untroubled,
In my breast—serpents lie!

The poem's structure is based on a series of relative clauses in which the poet describes himself in the third person, followed by dramatic self-revelation, skillfully placed at different parts of the two stanzas. The reader is addressed familiarly. He is implicitly identified with the crowd, whose opposition to the poet is second in importance only to the poet's preoccupation with himself. The poet-crowd opposition, a commonplace of romantic poetry, was used repeatedly with great dramatic intensity

[25] *Вариант:* «На коем фрак». *Примечание К. Пруткова.*
[26] Variant: "Who's wearing clothes." Note by K. Prutkov.

by both Puškin and Lermontov.[27] Here, however, it takes second place
to the poet's description of himself and is thus reduced to comic insignificance. The epithets used to describe the poet abound in hackneyed
romantic images: the gloomy brow, compared hyperbolically to the
foggy Kazbek; the hair in disarray; the nervous distraction, here shown
in its physical symptoms. The Prutkovian touch of the variant with the
exactly opposite meaning not only parodies the penchant of contemporary poets to publish various versions of their poems, but also proves
ingeniously that these epithets are interchangeable, therefore meaningless. The entire poem is built upon incongruities juxtaposed by rhyme
and meter, and not perceived by the "poet" himself. The naked poet
and the official in his frock-coat are both romantic figures to Prutkov;
each secretly nourishes the serpent in his breast. The romantic epithets
are undercut by such words as "nag" or "nervičeskij". This poem is
composed of a series of absurd contradictions— the pliant back (in
English the bent knee is the symbol of servitude) which does not bend,
the smile which conceals a serpent— skillfully subordinated to the greatest
contradiction of all, that the poet's prestige can be undermined not only
by the Philistine crowd, but also ultimately by his own nervous behavior.

"My Portrait" is an excellent example of the way Prutkovian parody
works, and the first two lines illustrate its technique in miniature. In the
long line the traditions of the genre are built up. In the short line with
its variant they are demolished. The reader is lulled into familiar responses
by some words and these are cut short by others. Thus disbelief, no
longer suspended, comes crashing to the ground. As in "Junker Schmidt",
metaphor becomes concrete. The reader sees the crowd actually snatching
a real laurel wreath from the poet's forehead. Connotation merges with
denotation when parody calls the tune.

The proud but dismal figure of the poet recurs constantly in Prutkov's
poetry, both in general and in specific parody. Further reminders of
Puškin occur in "My Inspiration" ("Moe vdoxnovenie"). It begins with
the line "Guljaju l' odin ja po Letnemu sadu", an obvious echo of
Puškin's "Brožu li ja vdol' ulic šumnyx", but continues with Prutkov's
own peculiar similes: comparing the poet's thoughts to midges swarming
over warm water; the poet to Attila, wounding with his inspired verse;
and finally comparing him to a cloud, making itself "gloomier and
gloomier" and suddenly bursting forth with verses over the throng.
It ends the long series of galloping amphibrachs and images of motion

[27]   See especially "Poet i tolpa" and "Poetu" by Puškin; "Poet" and "Prorok" by
Lermontov.

with the words "ja diko smejus' " ('I savagely laugh'). They seem abrupt both because they bring all motion to a halt and because they are unmotivated.

Vladimir Žemčužnikov, who wrote "My Inspiration", also composed another long romantic parody entitled "To the Throng" ("K tolpe"). Žemčužnikov's parody sometimes relies more on long-winded metaphor, as opposed to the shorter, sharper lines of Tolstoj in "Junker Schmidt" and "My Portrait"; but were it not for positive manuscript evidence of authorship, in some cases supported by references in letters, it would be impossible to determine authorship on stylistic criteria alone, so alike are the themes and styles employed by the two.

"To the Throng" again opposes the multitude to the scornful poet. Here the crowd is addressed outright in stilted rhetorical syntax and Church Slavonic diction:

> Клейми, клейми, толпа, в чаду сует всечасных,
> Из низкой зависти, мой громоносный стих:

> Stigmatize, oh throng, stigmatize in the fumes of hourly vanity
> From low envy my thunderbearing verse:

As with most Prutkovian verse, the poem is loaded with unforgettable parodic images, the most memorable of which is his "leaden verse" ("svincovyj stix"), a parody of Lermontov's "iron verse" ("železnyj stix"), later copied by Benediktov.[28] The rhetorical repetitions are themselves parodied in an almost Majakovskian self-mocking bombast: .

> Я вечно буду петь и песней наслаждаться,
> Я вечно буду пить чарующий нектар.

> I will sing eternally and revel in the song,
> I will drink eternally the enchanting nectar.

The exclamations which structure the poem turn on themselves in a pun, but in so doing gain new strength, just as they do in Futurist poetry.

Prutkov's creators detected a note of condescension lurking under the wounded defiance of the romantic hero, and this trait meshed perfectly with the natural attitude of Prutkov, of the bureaucrat for the "civilian world". In a poem entitled "From Koz'ma Prutkov to the Reader in a Moment of Frankness and Repentance" ("Ot Koz'my Prutkova k čita-

---

[28] Sukiasova, p. 160.

telju v minutu otkrovennosti i raskajanija"), Prutkov's previously-noted obsession with explaining himself to the reader is transmuted into the poet explaining to the vain, worldly "profane" reader what it means to be a poet. A poet is one "who gazes with laughter upon the tears of the unhappy" ("kto s smexom na slezy nesčastnyx vziraet"). In "unintentional" synaesthesia the inhuman egotism of the romantic poet is parodied. The mockery becomes progressively more evident in each stanza. In the sixth, the poet's verse is "high-sounding, thund'rous, although without meaning". In the seventh stanza, the poet, growing even more confiding, tells the reader not to fear poets when he meets them, although "we raise ourselves proudly above your heads", for "otherwise who would distinguish us in a crowd?" Thus the romantic hero confides in a moment of frankness that it is all a pose. Here we have poetry close to satire, for the behavior of the personage himself is mocked. This satire, however, is underscored in Prutkov's works by parody, which is concerned with verbal posing. As Tynjanov expressed it in one of his sharp punning formulations: "Parody ... turns the poetic speech-transaction ("poetičeskoe rečevedenie") into the speech behavior ("rečevoe povedenie") of the poet; underlining his position, it turns it into a pose."[29]

The romantic poet, although defiant to his fellow man, has deep feelings of insignificance and uncertitude when facing nature. His proud self-assurance in the human world gives way to perplexity and even anguish. He projects his own personality into nature and finds his fate enigmatically reflected therein. In the poem entitled "Before the Sea of Life" ("Pered morem žitejskim"), which, a footnote tells us, Koz'ma Prutkov wrote "in a moment of despair and turmoil à propos of the coming government reforms", the poet stands on a rock, ready to throw himself into the sea. The title tells us that the sea is the metaphorical sea of life (the phrase occurs in the Russian Orthodox funeral service) with all its worldly temptations. The last two lines realize the metaphor by bringing it firmly on to dry land: "The grasshopper leaps/But where, he sees not." The poet is now transmuted into a grasshopper, blindly hopping around. The absurdly shifting images and the colloquial language ("Daj-ka brošus' v more") enhance the humor of the poet's situation, but the main element of humor remains the assumption that real things can be seen metaphorically without any poetic help.

The absence of a logical connection between man's inner self and the outer world of nature can be stated in a number of ways. In good roman-

---

[29] Ju. N. Tynjanov, *Mnimaja poezija* (Moscow–Leningrad: Academia, 1931), p. 5.

tic poetry an emotional link is forged between the two. Prutkovian parody
simply presents unconnected phenomena, turning romantic anguish into
unmotivated humorous behavior. We can see this process most clearly
in Prutkov's Heine poems, generally considered parodies not of Heine
himself but of his lesser Russian disciples. Heine imitators ran rampant
in Russia in the 1840's and 1850's.[30] In England the Heine craze called
forth such parody as Rudyard Kipling's "Commonplaces" and H. C.
Bunner's "Imitation", an epigram which proclaimed:

> The German style of poem
> Is uncommonly popular now;
> For the worst of us poets can do it—
> Since Heine showed us how.[31]

This is precisely what Koz'ma Prutkov proceeds to demonstrate in his
four poems, first published in 1854, which bore such subtitles as "from
Heine", "an imitation of Heine", and "as though from Heine". We have
already seen a transmutation of Heine in "Junker Schmidt"; in the other
three poems—"At the Seashore", "Valiant Studiosuses", and "A Memory of Bygone Days"—we find somewhat less of Heine himself (although
much more than has been suggested by critics to date), but much of what
was taken to resemble Heine: the poem presenting a small slice of experience condensed into a few quatrains, the psychological parallelism between man and nature, the perplexity of man in his "ironic" situation and
the ending in a *pointe*, like that of telling Junker Schmidt that summer
will return. Aleksej Tolstoj had great respect for Heine himself. He translated more of his poetry than that of any other poet and remarked in
a letter to Sofija Andreevna in 1856 (after he had written some of the
parodies): "I have reread Heine and find that he is a true poet and a remarkable poet—and extraordinarily original."[32] But the pseudo-Heine
that Prutkov created would pay a greater, if left-handed, tribute to the
German poet than would good translations of the original.

The poem entitled "At the Seashore" ("Na vzmor'e") presents a small
drama in narrative form, a tale with echoes of the poor heroine—rich
oppressor theme of the romantic ballad, already turned to irony in
Puškin's "The Station-Master". Both its verse form and, in part, its
content possibly contain elements of parody of Lermontov's "Vozdušnyj

[30] See: A. Fedorova, "Russkij Gejne", *Russkaja poezija XIX veka* (Leningrad: Academia, 1929), pp. 248-98.
[31] Carolyn Wells, *A Parody Anthology* (New York: Scribners, 1932), p. 96.
[32] A. K. Tolstoj, *Sobranie sočinenij*, IV, 92.

korabl' " ("The Aerial Ship")[33] in which Napoleon rises from the grave and sails magically to France:

> На нем треугольная шляпа
> И серый походный сюртук.

> Wearing a three-cornered hat
> And a gray battle coat.

He calls his men, receives no answer, and sails back. Such words as "tjažko vzdyxaet" and "maxnuvši rukoju" are echoed in the deep sigh and arm-waving of Prutkov's gardener. Napoleon's bitter tears drop (kapajut) and the gardener picks (kopaet) his nose. Prutkov's rollicking amphibrachs and loosely rhymed quatrains bear the stamp of Tolstoj, but Vladimir Žemčužnikov collaborated in writing it. The sea, contrary to its prominence it the title, shrinks in the poem to a more backdrop, and the hero who stands alone at the end strikes a rather undignified pose.

НА ВЗМОРЬЕ

> На взморье, у самой заставы,
> Я видел большой огород.
> Растет там высокая спаржа;
> Капуста там скромно растет.

> Там утром всегда огородник
> Лениво проходит меж гряд;
> На нем неопрятный передник;
> Угрюм его пасмурный взгляд.

> Польет он из лейки капусту;
> Он спаржу небрежно польет;
> Нарежет зеленого луку
> И после глубоко вздохиет.

> Намедни к нему подъезжает
> Чиновник на тройке лихой.
> Он в теплых, высоких галошах;
> На шее лорнет золотой.

> «Где дочка твоя?» — вопрошает
> Чиновник, прищурясь в лорнет.
> Но, дико взглянув, огородник
> Махнул лишь рукою в ответ.

[33] This has been suggested by Hugh McLean.

И тройка назад поскакала,
Сметая с капусты росу...
Стоит огородник угрюмо
И пальцем копает в носу.

AT THE SEASHORE

Right up at the gates by the seashore,
I saw a large garden below.
The lofty asparagus grows there;
There cabbages modestly grow.

And there every morning the gardener
Goes lazily round twixt the beds;
And wearing a messy old apron;
Looks sullen and gloomy ahead.

He waters a pot on the cabbage;
And on the asparagus dry;
He cuts off the green of the onion
And afterwards heaves a deep sigh.

But lately to him in a troika
Comes riding a bureaucrat bold.
All dressed up in warm high galoshes,
And wearing a lorgnette of gold.

"Oh, where is your daughter?"—so questions
The bureaucrat, scrunching his eyes,
But, looking quite savage, the gardener
Just flung out his arm in reply.

And backwards the troika it gallops,
The dew from the cabbage it blows...
The gardener stands looking sullen
And silently picking his nose.

The mysterious little drama is presented through the eyes of an unidentified eavesdropping witness. Presumably much has gone before, but it remains shrouded in mystery. The setting and characters are marvelously grotesque. Nature takes the form of a truck-garden with "tall asparagus". The protagonists are: the sullen gardener, in a messy apron, a sort of debased folk hero; the dashing figure of the bureaucrat (a contradiction in terms to anyone but Prutkov) wearing "galoši" (a quaint word in Russian) who, arriving in an almost supernatural troika, interrupts the idyllic scene; and the gardener's daughter who never appears. Presumably some violence has been done, of which the troika sweeping the dew from the cabbage (the poetic from the prosaic) is a symbol. The poem is based on a series of disconnected actions, but in humorous as opposed to romantic poetry no effort need be made to connect these actions.

"The Valiant Studiosuses" ("Doblestnye studiozusy"—an archaic German word for student with a Russian plural ending) concerns two quarreling German students and their inability to understand a feeble pun of the narrator. They too "stand in meditation" at the end. The poem probably parodies the arrogance of the narrator, who forces the reader to applaud his pun, as much as the thick-headed German students. As in many poems by Heine, the narrator has to choose between two men (for instance, a rabbi and a moula) and finds their similarities greater than their difference.

The final pseudo-Heine poem, "A Memory of Bygone Days" ("Pamjat' prošlogo"), may have been inspired by a poem by Benediktov, "Ja pomnju", written in 1857.[34] But only the first line resembles Benediktov's original "Ja pomnju: byla ty rebenkom." The meditative final couplet and the construction by contrasts relate this poem more to the other pseudo-Heine ones than to any parodies of Benediktov.[35] The poem has a charmingly humorous, erotic nostalgia:

ПАМЯТЬ ПРОШЛОГО
КАК БУДТО ИЗ ГЕЙНЕ

Помню я тебя ребенком,
Скоро будет сорок лет;
Твой передничек измятый,
Твой затянутый корсет.

Было в нем тебе неловко;
Ты сказала мне тайком:
«Распусти корсет мне сзади;
Не могу я бегать в нем».

Весь исполненный волненья,
Я корсет твой развязал. . .
Ты со смехом убежала,
Я ж задумчиво стоял.

---

[34] This has been suggested by Berkov, *Koz'ma Prutkov*, p. 547.
[35] Heine's own poem "An Jenny" (Heine, II, 361-62) has a similar ironic nostalgia.

A MEMORY OF BYGONE DAYS

AS THOUGH FROM HEINE

I remember you in childhood,
Almost forty years ago;
With your rumpled pinafore on,
With your corset laced in so.

In it you were feeling awkward;
As you told me secretly:
"Let my corset out in back now;
In it I cannot run free."

All suffused with agitation,
I your corset then unwound;
You ran off with happy laughter,
I stood still in thought profound.

The quasi-pathetic forty-year-old memory of a trivial incident is fraught with metaphysical anxiety and erotic day-dreaming. The poem has an almost unconscious quality to it, which adds to its humor. As T. S. Eliot remarked, "the bad poet is usually unconscious where he ought to be conscious and conscious where he ought to be unconscious. Both errors tend to make him 'personal'."[36] The trivial personal incident, isolated from the rest of life, exaggerated emotionally, often shrouded in enigma, is contrasted, usually implicitly, to reality in the "Heine" poems. The same technique is used in Prutkov's poetry of a more specifically parodic nature.

If one figure above all must be selected as the poet most thoroughly parodied in the poetry of Koz'ma Prutkov, then that unfortunate man would be V. G. Benediktov. Even their biographies are similar: Benediktov too served in the army, but left it for the Ministry of Finance where he remained twenty-six years, eventually attaining the rank of general. His parallel literary career consisted of seven years of dizzy fame, followed by seventy of jeering ridicule. In 1835, his verse was first published in a slim, one hundred and eight page volume of forty-eight poems, and in just half a year the second edition came out. In two years, twenty-nine new poems were published with equal success. All Russia declaimed "Kudri" ("Curls").[37] But in 1842 when his third collection

---

[36] T. S. Eliot, "Tradition and the Individual Talent", *Selected Essays* (New York: Harcourt, Brace and Company, 1950), p. 10.
[37] I. N. Rozanov, *Literaturnye reputacii* (Moscow, 1928), p. 72.

of verse was published, all the writers in Russia seemed to criticize his verse and his life.

Critical opinion is still divided about him today, but he cannot be ignored—only partly because Koz'ma Prutkov put him in a permanent spotlight. Benediktov's detractors accused him of keeping the trappings of romanticism "borrowed in a simplified way ... having lost the direct link with the philosophical sources."[38] On the other hand, Benediktov's innovations, his daring use of catachresis, and his neologisms have been appreciated by some critics. Julij Aixenval'd writes of Benediktov's poems:

> They were composed, perhaps ... in a fit of sincere, not cold, ecstasy; but in any case their form is somehow separate from content and mood, the form stands out and speaks of itself and shines and overflows into space in waves of sound. With Benediktov, the flesh of the word becomes independent of its soul. His verses are very beautiful and decorative, although often banal. But, themselves soulless, they do not touch the soul of others.[39]

Tolstoj and the Žemčužnikovs seized upon the unnaturalness of Benediktov, his theoretical kind of romantic ecstasy; but they matched him in verbal innovation, turning it into a comic feature.

The poem entitled "Poezdka v Kronštadt" ("Journey to Kronstadt"), dedicated to Benediktov, parodies his language above all, although it ends in a parody of the self-pitying poet. The first four quatrains describing the steamship's journey are excellent imitations of the poetic richness of Benediktov at his best:

> Пена клубом. Пар клокочет.
> Брызги перлами летят.
> У руля матрос хлопочет.
> Мачты в воздухе торчат.

> Foam puffs. Steam boils up.
> Spray flies like pearls.
> The sailor is busy at the rudder
> The masts jut out in the air.

Clumsy lines follow, jolting the reader into laughter by comparison. The following quatrains abound in such rhetorical repetitions as:

[38]   L. Ja. Ginzburg, preface to V. G. Benediktov, *Stikotvorenija* (Leningrad, 1939), p. xii.
[39]   Ju. I. Ajxenval'd, *Siluety russkix pisatelej* (Moscow, 1910), III, 37.

На носу один стою я,
И стою я как утес.
Морю песни в честь пою я,
И пою я не без слез.

On the prow alone I stand,
And I stand like a rock.
Songs to honor the sea I sing,
And I sing not without tears.

The last three words were changed from "veseljas' " for the *Complete Works*, to make the phrase even more tongue- and thought-twisting. In the last stanzas the steamship, once in the bay, hangs its head, looking at the vainly bustling people, in a weird personification. The poem is a comic "Bateau ivre" *avant la lettre*. Its companion piece "Vozvraščenie in Kronštadta" ("Return from Kronstadt") is less daringly like a Benediktov poem and so it fails comparatively as parody.

Prutkov's longest poem "Akvilon" ("The Aquilon") is also dedicated "to the memory of Mr. Benediktov" and parodies his poem "More" ("The Sea") with its use of three different meters in one poem. Prutkov, more conservative, only uses two. The change in meter has no apparent motivation in Benediktov, but Prutkov used it to illustrate the poet's sudden change of mind at the end, when he decides to row to safety. Prutkov counters such Benediktovian epithets as "Beloparusnyj, plavučij/Volnoborec-vodorez!" with his own:

То был плаватель могучий,
Крутобедрый гений вод,
Трехмачтовый град плавучий,
Стосаженный скороход.

This was a mighty swimmer,
A steep-hipped genius of the waters,
A triple-masted swimming city,
A seven hundred foot long speeder.

Prutkov's poem contains some word-for-word repetitions of Benediktov, but his own parodic inventions à la Benediktov are even more successful.

Benediktov's best-known poem "Kudri" ("Curls") is an elaborate synecdoche. He heaped up metaphors to describe the sight, smell, and feel of hair, whose owner is never mentioned, and then continues asking, in a series of erotic images, whose hand will possess the curls. Prutkov follows this structure exactly, but substitutes a prosaic neck for romantic curls. His metaphors are even more preposterous, although as heavily Church Slavonicized, and they do everything but describe their subject. There are two extant drafts of the poem, and in the second the epithets are even more exaggerated and indicate action as well as repose:

> Шея девы — наслажденье;
> Шея — снег, змея, нарцис;
> Шея — ввысь порой стремленье;
> Шея — склон порою вниз.

> The neck of a maiden is bliss;
> The neck is snow, a serpent, Narcissus;
> The neck at times straining upwards
> The neck at times inclined downwards.

Prutkov is generally less erotic than Benediktov; he asks who will keep mosquitoes and dust off the neck. The best humorous effects are achieved when, finally, corporeal synecdoche becomes disembodiment.

Another poet much and cruelly parodied in his verse and in his person was A. A. Fet, whom Prutkov called "Ibn Fet" thereby emphasizing his remoteness from contemporary Russia; but Prutkov's two parodies are so full of comic insight that one forgets that Fet, unlike Benediktov, was concerned with kinds of perception to the point where his questionings of experience were genuine. In Prutkov's poems Fet's *persona* becomes a lazy, bored man, and his attempts to understand anything are ridiculed. In the poem "Osen' " ("Autumn"), vague yearnings are undercut by the last line:

> Осень. Скучно. Ветер воет.
> Мелкий дождь по окнам льет.
> Ум тоскует; сердце ноет;
> И душа чего-то ждет.

> И в бездейственном покое
> Нечем скуку мне отвесть...
> Я не знаю: что такое?
> Хоть бы книжку мне прочесть!

> Autumn. Boredom. Wind is wailing
> Small rain patters on the pane.
> Mind is anguished; heart is ailing;
> Soul awaits something in vain.

In my comfortable inertia
Boredom looms where'er I look.
I don't know, what is the matter?
Wish that I could read a book!

The poem "Autumn" is what Grossman termed "an ironic cross-section"[40] of much of Fet's poetry. As the commentary of B. Ja. Buxštab points out, it most resembles a poem by Fet beginning with the words:

Непогода — осень — куришь,
Куришь — всё как будто мало.
Хоть читал бы, — только чтенье
Подвигается так вяло.

Bad weather—fall—you smoke,
You smoke—everything seems little
Wish I could read—only reading
Progresses so sluggishly.

Buxštab further demonstrates that the line: "Ja ne znaju, čto takoe" is from the early redaction of Fet's poem "Letnij večer tix i jasen" ("The summer evening is quiet and clear"). But the parody is probably even more general; Prutkov's guardians obviously read much of what Fet wrote in the 1860's and before. Fet's poetry is full of such lines as: "Kak mne pečal' prevozmoč'?" ("How can I overcome my sadness?"), "Čego xoču?" ("What do I want?"), and "Čem toske, i ne znaju, pomoč' " ("And I do not know how to help my anguish").[41] Prutkov's parody takes metaphysical boredom and traces its cause to inactivity. He answers the anguished questions of Fet's *persona* comically by destroying their cosmic frame of reference and reducing them to the idle musings of a pampered man.

The other Prutkovian Fet poem, written by Aleksej Žemčužnikov in 1883, parodied a poem by Fet "V dymke-nevidimke",[42] written ten years earlier and published in his collection *Večernie ogni* that same year. The title "Flashes in the Dark" ("Blestki vo t'me") parodies not only the title of Fet's collection but also his style of short, flashing images, suggesting a mood rather than stating it. Finally, Prutkov may have

---

[40] L. P. Grossman, "Parodija kak žanr literaturnoj kritiki", in *Russkaja literaturnaja parodija* (Moscow, 1930), p. 47.
[41] All quotations are from A. A. Fet, *Polnoe sobranie sočinenij* (Leningrad, 1959). The lines are from pp. 167, 182 and 287.
[42] *Ibid.*, p. 187.

been referring to Fet's view of the illuminating function of art in this pungent title; if so, his inventors, judging from their own poetry and aesthetic position, would be less critical of Fet's aesthetics than of the poetic hesitations and uncertainties of his *persona*. Comparing the two poems, we may see how the parody works:

Над плакучей ивой	Above the weeping willow
Утренняя зорька...	Morning light...
А в душе тоскливо	And in the soul weariness,
И во рту так горько.	And in the mouth bitterness.
Дворик постоялый	The little inn
На большой дороге...	On the main road...
А в душе усталой	And in the tired soul
Тайные тревоги.	Secret anxieties.
На озимом поле	In the winterfield
Псовая охота...	Hunting with dogs...
А на сердце боли	And in the heart more pain
Больше отчего-то.	For some reason.
В синеве небесной	In the blue of the sky
Пятнышка не видно...	Not a speck in sight...
Почему ж мне тесно?	Why am I feeling cramped?
Отчего ж мне стыдно?	Wherefore am I ashamed?
Вот я снова дома;	Here I am home again:
Убрано роскошно...	It is decorated luxuriously...
А в груди истома	But in my breast languor
И как будто тошно!	And, as it were, nausea.
Свадебные брашна,	Wedding Feasts,
Шутка-прибаутка...	Jest and sally...
Отчего ж мне страшно?	Wherefore am I afraid?
Почему ж мне жутко?	Why am I terrified?
	(Prutkov)
В дымке-невидимке	In the invisible haze
Выплыл месяц вешний,	The spring moon floated forth,
Цвет садовый дышит	The garden flower breathes
Яблонью, черешней.	With apple, with cherry,
Так и льнет, целуя	And thus it clings, kissing
Тайно и нескромно.	Secretly and boldly.
И тебе не грустно?	And are you not sad?
И тебе не томно?	And are you not languid?

Истерзался песней	The nightingale without the rose
Соловей без розы.	Was tormented with song.
Плачет старый камень	The old stone weeps,
В пруд роняя слезы.	Dropping tears into the pond.
Уронила косы	The head unwillingly
Голова неволью.	Dropped its braids.
И тебе не томно?	And are you not languid?
И тебе не больно?	And are you not pained?

(Fet)

Prutkov's parody atomizes the structure of Fet's poem. Calling the descriptive lines A and the interrogative lines B, we have in Fet 6 A plus 2 B twice and in Prutkov 2 A plus 2 B six times. Fet's interlocutor is unspecified, Prutkov's *persona* is talking to himself. In Fet's poem, nature is connected to the poet's feelings by personifying verbs; in Prutkov's there is absolutely no connection between the first and last two lines of each quatrain, so that the anguish of the *persona* becomes increasingly more comic with each repetition, in a perfect illustration of Bergson's theory of comic repetition. Prutkov gives additional details of trivial human actions, some directly referring to Fet (such as "psovaja oxota", a poem by him and also the subject of an early poem by Nekrasov, and the reference to the comfortable surroundings on the estate Fet worked so long to acquire). The quatrains increase in meaninglessness, but if read backwards, they suggest that the hero has a "real" cause for his anguish: he has been at a wedding (his own?), has eaten and drunk too much, and is afraid of the life ahead. The parody may seem like unnecessary cruelty to a great poet who led a difficult life, but good parody, like good poetry, is its own justification. It attacks Fet on his own grounds, imitating his style as well as mocking it. Except for a few of the many parodies of Fet by D. D. Minaev (who had the brilliant idea of writing one of Fet's poems backwards, hardly changing its content thereby),[43] Prutkov's two parodies are the most acute and enjoyable today. Most of the other Fet parodies were really satires, and we remember Fet for his poetry, not his polemics.

There exists a single parody on a contemporary of Fet, Ja. P. Polonskij, which again both parodies a single work "The Finnish Coast" ("Finskij bereg") and characterizes much of Polonskij's favorite ballad style. The ballad tells a story and Prutkov's parody, called "Disenchantment" ("Razočarovanie") reproduces the meter, rhyme scheme, length, and dialogue form of the original poem, and even parodies the story itself.

---

[43] In Tynjanov, *Mnimaja poezija*, p. 316.

In both poems the narrator is an outsider and fails in the dialogue to communicate with a girl. But in Prutkov's poem the questioning has a "Father William"-like ring to it. The narrator follows the girl around on her household chores until she finally loses patience at stupid questions and insults him. Then he remarks how "we often childishly love what is unworthy of attention". This poem also contains a hint of parody of the intellectual hero with book and beer in hand who tries to communicate with a folk heroine and only bothers her.

Several of Prutkov's other poems are wholly devoted to the Slavophiles and their associates—especially to Xomjakov, Ivan Aksakov and Apollon Grigor'ev. None, perhaps, attains the perfection of "In the Album of a Beautiful Foreigner". The other Slavophile poems depend more on the reader's knowledge that they are parodies of Slavophile concepts as well as writings. Parody has a parasitic nature. Since the Slavophiles were less good as poets, Prutkov had no richness to feed on as he had in the cases of Benediktov or Fet, and the resulting parody was somewhat less rich.

"A Contemporary Russian Song" ("Sovremennaja russkaja pesn' ") mocks the central tenet of the Slavophile creed, a belief in the great worth of the Russian people. It parodies folk poetry: the use of dactyllic endings, participial forms in či, and syntactical parallels. The content consists of a series of left-handed praises for Russian food and Russian customs, followed by explanations for Russian laziness: "We would work, but the will isn't there;/We would be happy to, but don't want to." They prefer to praise Russia, as did the Slavophiles.

Prutkov's other Slavophile poetry, more parodic and less satirical than this, selects themes from specific writings of certain Slavophile poets. In the poem "Native Things" ("Rodnoe") the target is still the crude ways of country people and especially their language, but it refers in part to "Brodjaga", a poem written by Ivan Aksakov. Prutkov's poem begins idylically enough, describing the peace the narrator finds watching the people at their daily tasks—planting, road-building and weaving—but then he tells how he loves to hear native swearing, and the poem erupts into name-calling peasant dialogue. In the *Complete Works* the poem is considerably shortened; it takes only a few lines to get the idea.

If the Slavophiles aspired to closeness to the folk, their other great dream was to become one with nature. Prutkov parodies Xomjakov's "A Wish" ("Želanie") in his "Wishes of the Poet" ("Želanija poeta"), fragmenting Xomjakov's single philosophical desire into a plural series of ridiculous metamorphoses. Prutkov changed what Xomjakov probably understood to be a wish of all mankind to a personal desire of the poet. Whereas Xomjakov starts with the general wish of pouring himself out into the world ("Xotel by ja razlit'sja v mire"), Prutkov begins with the perhaps equally preposterous but much more particular wish of wanting to be a tulip ("Xotel by ja tjul'panum byt' "). "Tulip", in Russian, is a foreign-sounding word as well. Both poems contain a series of transmutations of the poet, but Xomjakov's similes (he would like to be a butterfly) become Prutkov's concrete aspirations. Again the metaphor is made literal. Finally, while Xomjakov talks about being "in the world" and "in nature" ("*v* prirode"), Prutkov would like to "stray about the world" ("*po* prirode"), not losing himself in it, but on the contrary, playing capricious games with nature. Prutkov treats Slavophile aspirations as the irresponsible and egotistical fantasies of the romantic poet in Russian disguise.

In another parody of Xomjakov, "My Dream" ("Moj son"), Prutkov takes the theme of a dream of death and the poet's immortality from two of Xomjakov's poems and the meter from a third. The alternation of long with very short lines provides a good vehicle for humorous punch lines. The poet fears he will fall asleep forever and wonders who will take his lyre. But then his dream becomes more and more glorious, as he sees himself crowned with laurel in heaven and seventeen columns arise over his ashes; but at the end cold reality returns when he awakens, still alive.

> Но — ах! — я проснулся, к несчастью, живой,
>   Здоровый!

> But—oh! I awakened, unfortunately, alive,
>   Healthy!

Immortality will have to wait.

When Prutkov wrote a long poem parodying Apollon Grigor'ev, his critique was of a different order. He ridiculed Grigor'ev's critical terminology[44] (which had more than once been unfavorably directed to the comedies of Aleksej Žemčužnikov, although he was the only one who appreciated *Fantasia*) by tearing it out of its former context and stirring it thickly into one poem. "An Impossible Situation" ("Bezvyxodnoe položenie") takes the title of an autobiographical work by Grigor'ev

---

[44] For a list of this terminology and its origins, see: Koz'ma Prutkov, ed. Berkov, pp. 536-37.

and is a pastiche on Grigor'ev's difficult-to-follow writings. It describes, in a sort of confessional style, the difficulties and problems of literary criticism as Grigor'ev practiced it. The most damning lines are:

> И технике пустой не слишком предаваясь,
> Я тщился разъяснить творения процесс
> И «слово новое» сказать в своем созданьи!. .

> And not indulging overly in empty technique
> I endeavoured to explain the process of creation
> And speak a "new word" in my work!. . .

The "empty technique" probably refers to Grigor'ev's alleged disregard for the poetic technique of others. His immodest efforts to explain the mystery of the creative process is further undercut by the desire to be new and original. Grigor'ev's defense of Ostrovskij had been reinforced by a somewhat melodramatic defense of the critical terms he himself had used to describe Ostrovskij's art. (" 'A new word'—I now employ with some pride that expression whose grandiloquence has been compromised by the frivolous or malicious laughing-stock into which it has been turned...").[45] But Prutkov turns his persona, a transparent parody of Grigor'ev, into someone not only ambitious and defensive, but also confused. The persona becomes entangled in his own concepts and the poem leaves him trying to find a way out of his own plan. This is a parody of criticism as an art, and Russian literature would have been enriched had there been more good parody of critics and their styles. Grigor'ev is mocked for his lack of clarity, his new, "scientific" terminology, his penchant for imprinting his "inner 'I' " on the material at hand, and for constructing an "ideal" from the categories he has invented. The ideal concepts and murky style of Grigor'ev's critical articles, like those of Slavophile poetry, are parodied in Prutkov's poetry as just another extension of the romantic ego.

While the Slavophiles, with their purely Russian romanticism, abhorred things foreign, other neo-romantics rushed to embrace the poetry they saw in Greece, Germany, or Spain. Hispanic genres were not so far removed from Slavophile poetry, as Prutkov's parodies proved. More highly stylised, but just as little reasoned as Slavophile poetry, these poems were still exotic outgrowths of the *Russian* soil. If the Russian

---

[45] A. A. Grigor'ev, *Polnoe sobranie sočinenij i pisem* (Petrograd, 1918), I, 214. Grigor'ev had used this term earlier in his favorable review of Gogol''s *Selected Passages from Correspondence with Friends.*

Slavophiles could romanticize their own people, the Russian anthologists could romanticize the Greeks.

In the 1840's in Russia, the Protean creature that was neo-romanticism had gone so far as to take pseudo-classical shapes, and Prutkov therefore did not neglect to write, in addition to his play "The Dispute of the Ancient Greek Philosophers", poetry in a style of romantic Hellenism—the so-called anthological genre whose best-known representatives were the poets Majkov and Ščerbina. This poetry usually has a conventional ancient Greece as its setting. The narrator is supposed to be less impassioned than the romantic as he gazes at what lies around him. He sees not the violent motion of a stormy sea, but more static landscapes: people in statuesque poses, harmonious and composed backgrounds. He savors the beautiful details of the world surrounding him. But Prutkov caught the same aloofness, the same lofty disdain in the pose of the neo-classic that he had mocked in the neo-romantic.

The poem entitled "The Ancient Plastic Greek" ("Drevnij plastičeskij grek") is a perfect example of a parody of the anthological genre as a whole, as well as of critics like A. V. Družinin who fostered the use of such terms as "plastic" to describe its images.[46]

Люблю тебя, дева, когда золотистый
И солнцем облитый ты держишь лимон,
И юноши зрю подбородок пушистый
Меж листьев аканфа и белых колонн.

Красивой хламиды тяжелые складки
    Упали одна за другой . .
Так в улье шумящем, вкруг раненой матки,
    Снует озабоченный рой.

I love you, my sweet girl, whenever you're holding
A fine golden lemon, all drenched in the light,
The soft downy chin of a youth I'm beholding
Twixt leaves of acantha and columns of white.

The loose, heavy pleats of the beautiful chlamys
    One after the other fell free...
And thus in the beehive around their hurt queen press
    The swarms of solicitous bees.

The amphibrachic poem is based on a series of *non sequiturs*. Up to a point they could be attributed to a fragmentation of attention on the

46 Sukiasova, pp. 169-70.

part of the persona, who does not know what to admire most. The word "tak", however, introduces a simile connecting the two parts of the final quatrain. The poet, that sensual observer of separate details of the world, loses his way in concepts that might explain them. His poetic equipment consists not of metaphor but of rhyme, some Greek words and what are called in Russian *ukrašajuščie epitety*, adjectives frequently neutral in meaning which serve only to decorate the noun they modify. Nearly every noun in this poem has such an adjective; Prutkov sought thereby to insure the "beauty" of his poem.

Prutkov wrote two parodies specifically of Ščerbina (Greek on his mother's side), who wrote poems about ancient and modern Greece in the 1850's and then in the 1860's wrote mainly satirical verse. Prutkov's "Letter from Corinth" ("Pis'mo iz Korinfa") parodies "A Letter" ("Pis'mo") of Ščerbina, published in his collection *Grečeskie stixotvorenija* in 1850. Ščerbina's poem describes a lazy, sensual life in the Boeotian countryside and concludes with the lines:

> Только слухом живу я да зреньем...
> Красота, красота, красота! —
> Я одно лишь твержу с умиленьем.

> By sound and sight alone I live...
> Beauty, beauty, beauty! —
> I repeat only this with tender emotion.

Such an exclamation contained too much raw emotion for Prutkov's mentors, who also parodied the conversational tone by making his own poem as awkward as possible. Written in the same meter, it begins:

> Я недавно приехал в Коринф.
> Вот ступени, а вот колоннада.
> Я люблю здешних мраморных нимф
> И истмийского шум водопада.

> I have recently come to Corinth.
> Here are steps and here is a colonnade.
> I love the local marble nymphs
> And the noise of the isthmus waterfall.

In a haphazard, clumsy way the poet records his impressions. The repetition of "vot", "zdešnij" applied to a marble nymph, the two "i" sounds in sequence, the adjective "istmijskij"— all contribute to the clumsiness. The poet lists a series of particularly Greek pastimes he enjoys, like rubbing his loins with olive-oil and enjoying slave-girls. Finally, he echoes the line about beauty: "Krasota! krasota!—vse tveržu ja." Ščerbina has so overstated his case that Prutkov's parody can even cut down the number of exclamations.

"The Philosopher in the Bath" ("Filosof v bane") parodies a poem Ščerbina wrote in which the poet, after being massaged, begins to philosophize about the soul's immortality. Prutkov tells the girl to stop massaging him, but just to tickle his bald head. That he is a philosopher is clear only from the title. The use of Greek decor to exploit a sensual theme is parodied in this glimpse of ancient Greeks at their toilette.

Contemporary as well as ancient Greece came into European consciousness during the War for Independence against the Turks. In 1824 C. Fauriel's book "Les chants populaires de la Grèce moderne" appeared and was translated into Russian by Gnedič. Later, in the 1840's and for twenty years afterwards "modern Greek songs" appeared in Russia, written by Majkov, Ščerbina, and others. Prutkov's contribution to this series was his "New Greek Song" ("Novogrečeskaja pesn' "), a sort of merry rondo with circular reasoning in it as well:

> Спит залив. Эллада дремлет.
> Под портик уходит мать
> Сок гранаты выжимать. . .
> Зоя! нам никто не внемлет!
> Зоя, дай себя обнять!
>
> Зоя, утренней порою
> Я уйду отсюда прочь;
> Ты смягчись, покуда ночь!
> Зоя, утренней порою
> Я уйду отсюда прочь. . .
>
> Пусть же вихрем сабля свищет!
> Мне Костаки не судья!
> Прав Костаки, прав и я!
> Пусть же вихрем сабля свищет;
> Мне Костаки не судья!
>
> В поле брани Разорваки
> Пал за вольность как герой.
> Бог с ним! рок его такой.
> Но зачем же жив Костаки,
> Когда в поле Разорваки
> Пал за вольность как герой?!

Видел я вчера в заливе
Восемнадцать кораблей;
Все без мачт и без рулей...
Но султана я счастливей;
Лей вина мне, Зоя, лей!

Лей, пока Эллада дремлет,
Пока тщетно тщится мать
Сок гранаты выжимать...
Зоя, нам никто не внемлет!
Зоя, дай себя обнять!

The gulf is sleeping. Hellas drowses.
Through porticoes your mother leaves
Pomegranate juice to squeeze...
Zoya! Not a soul it rouses!
Zoya! Come, embrace me, please!

Zoya, I from here must hasten
E'en before the night is spent;
While it's dark yet, please relent!
Zoya, I from here must hasten
E'en before the night is spent...

May my sword swish like a whirlwind!
Kostaki is no judge of me!
I am right and so is he!
May my sword swish like a whirlwind;
Kostaki is no judge of me!

In the battle Razorvaki
Fell a hero for free Greece.
That's his fate; God grant him peace.
But why is he alive, Kostaki,
When in battle Razorvaki
Fell a hero for free Greece?!

Yesterday in the gulf waters
Eighteen ships there did appear;
None had masts or helms to steer...
I'm happier still than a vizir;
Pour the wine out, Zoya, dear!

Pour, while all of Hellas drowses
Agreeably, mother now agrees
Pomegranate juice to squeeze...
Zoya, not a soul it rouses!
Zoya, come, embrace me, please!

The name Kostaki is taken from Ščerbina, but Razorvaki is, as we have seen, an original invention and an extremely successful pun to a Russian ear. The humor of the poem lies in its repetitions, in keeping with the lyric-epic style of the "pesn' " genre, but these refrains are completely meaningless. Thus, not only lines but also words ("prav") or even clusters of sounds ("tščetno tščitsja") are repeated, but the epic picture, with its confusing drama of dead and live heroes and the unconnected vision of rudderless ships in the gulf (a sign of Greek defeat) with its startling effect of unmotivated happiness in the hero is overpowered by the framework of the attempted seduction of Zoya. Wine, women, and bloody battle are the necessary ingredients of the neo-Greek pesn', and Prutkov made sure they were all present, swept up willy-nilly into the song.

Aleksej Žemčužnikov contributed two "Latin" poems to the collection of Prutkovian antiquity. "To an Ancient Greek Old Woman" ("Drevnej grečeskoj staruxe"), which continues the parody of the scornful persona, is called an "imitation of Catullus", but it really preserves the spirit of his poems about Mamurra, especially, we believe, one in which the poet attacks him indirectly by describing the unlovely traits of a girl of his, in what might be described as an elegy in reverse.[47] Prutkov's poem retains the graphic bawdiness of Catullus, but the poem is parodic in its hypothetical situation. A Roman (who would not call a Greek "ancient") spurns the old woman in the extremely hypothetical case that she would solicit his love. This said, however, Prutkov has composed a

[47] The poem by Catullus is as follows:

> Salve, nec minimo puella naso,
> nec bello pede nec nigris ocellis,
> nec longis digitis nec ore sicco,
> nec sane nimis elegante lingua,
> decoctoris amica Formiani.
> te provincia narrat esse bellam?
> tecum Lesbia nostra comparatur?
> o saeclum insapiens et infacetum!

[from "Catulli Carmina", in C. J. Fordyce, *Catullus: A Commentary* (Oxford: Clarendon Press, 1961), p. 23.] As Rolfe Humphries idiomatically renders it:

> Why, hello, little girl with the great big nose,
> Gawky feet and pallid, washed-out eyes,
> Stubby fingers, drooling mouth, and tongue
> Anything but elegant in expression;
> Girl-friend of the hick-town, hock-shop haunter!
> You're the one the province says is lovely?
> You're the one my darling is compared to?
> O, what a stupid, half-wit generation!

twelve-line poem of splendid vituperation in the Catullan style. Here the same tasteless subject of the lascivious old woman, as in *Ljubov' and Silin*, is made artistically pleasing in such well-balanced lines as "Pripomni blizkij Stiks i strasti pozabud'!," ("Be mindful of the nearing Styx and forget your passions!") mingled with the grotesque admonitions to cover her body. The poem like the Heine poems, proves how close good parody can come to imitation.

The other Latin poem, "Katerina", has an epigraph by Cicero, the beginning of his famous speech against Catiline: "Quousque tandem, Catilina, abutere patientia nostra?" The poem takes the form of a dialogue between the persona and a certain Katerina who abuses his patience by giving mundane replies to his declarations of love, taking his metaphors literally. But the chief charm of the poem lies in the racy meter, the rhymes in "ina" in every second line, such inner rhymes as "Ty kartina, Katerina", and most of all the utter nonsense of the Katerina-Catilina sound-simile. When a pun provides the impetus for a poem, it cannot strictly be called parody.

Two of Prutkov's other exotic lyrics fit this category of the predominance of sound over sense. (In general, however, we may note that puns, nonsense-words, and words used just for the sake of their sound occur far less frequently in Prutkov and generally in Russian literature before 1910 than they do in English literature). The untitled poem beginning "Na mjagkoj krovati" is called "a romance", which in Russian poetry had come to mean a short melodic poem, usually telling a tale of love in short, rhymed stanzas. Such poetry was easily set to music. In Prutkov's exotic setting, the recumbent narrator overhears a bloody incident involving a romantic triangle. The humor is derived not only from certain illogical images like that of a moon in an azure sky but also from absurd sounds: the "pif-paf" of a bullet and the hat with a tinsel cord ("s šnurom mišurnym")—obviously sound effects intended to add comically to the melodrama.

The poem "The Wish to be Spanish" "(Želanie byt' ispancem")" is a parody of the Spanish theme in Russian poetry which began back in 1789 with Karamzin's "Graf Gravinos" and continued into the 1860's. Still the parody of Spanish-sounding names, places, and objects in which the poem abounds seems to be superseded by a delight in the sounds for their own sake. The exotic setting this time frames the speaker's impassioned plea for the accoutrements of the Spaniard (including a mantilla, for he obviously does not know that this garment is worn by women only), containing a request for "unbounded jealousy/a cup of chocolate"—

all so that he can "sooner or later" take a silken ladder from his pocket and get the girl. It appears later that he is a monk and fears the Inquisition will denounce him. It is hard to name something Spanish that does not appear in this poem (although, again, some less successful quatrains about sherry and veils have been pruned out for the *Complete Works*), but everything is juxtaposed with something vastly different, just as the Spanish words are fitted into the Russian language by rhyme, almost as if they belonged there.

These poems, along with the punning fables, poems like "Neck", and numerous parts of other poems form a current of word-play in Prutkov's works, verbal nonsense which complements the situational or philosophical nonsense of his poetry. While Prutkov frequently uses words for their own sake, there is usually something more to the general (as opposed to the specifically parodic) humor of his poetry. In several poems, the nonsense current is verbally and situationally focused on one character who dominates the poem. Such is the case with Junker Schmidt, or the country neighbor who takes a nose-dive in the mud, or the man who will not stain his honor by falling in love with a foreigner, or the poet obsessed with the crowd. These characters create their own romantic or absurd situation. They have an idea they will not let go of and this *idée fixe* usually brings about their ruin.

In three of Prutkov's poems, the ballad and the chivalric romance serve as vehicles to carry three unforgettable Prutkovian knights, all obsessed with something and unwilling to explain why. Thus, Baron von Grinval'dus, "famed in Germany" in the poem "A German Ballad" ("Nemeckaja ballada") sits on a rock in front of a castle and says nothing. He may be patterned after a Schillerian knight, known in Russia through a translation by Žukovskij,[48] but Prutkov's knight, instead of dying for love in a cell, just sits for no reason "year after year . . . in the same position." The poem is structured on the repetitions and parallels of the ballad, but they also serve to reinforce the obsessive quality of the Baron's behavior, while a prosaic phrase like "v toj že pozic'i" deflates the romantically incantatory spell such repetitions weave.

A second Prutkovian knight is identified simply as "The Wayfarer" in the ballad "Putnik".

> Путник едет косогором;
> Путник по полю спешит.
> Он обводит тусклым взором
> Степи снежной грустный вид.

[48] Koz'ma Prutkov, p. 434.

«Ты к кому спешишь на встречу,
Путник гордый и немой?»
— «Никому я не отвечу:
Тайна то души больной!

Уж давно я тайну эту
Хороню в груди своей,
И бесчувственному свету
Не открою тайны сей:

Ни за знатность, ни за злато,
Ни за груды серебра,
Ни под взмахами булата,
Ни средь пламени костра!»

Он сказал — и вдаль несется
Косогором, весь в снегу.
Конь испуганный трясется,
Спотыкаясь на бегу.

Путник с гневом погоняет
Карабагского коня.
Конь усталый упадает,
Седока с собой роняет
И под снегом погребает
Господина и себя.

Схороненный под сугробом,
Путник тайну скрыл с собой.
Он пребудет и за гробом
Тот же гордый и немой.

The traveller rides o'er the hill;
Now he hastens through the fields;
Round he looks with glances dull
At the steppe in snow concealed.

"To what meeting do you hasten,
O wayfarer mute and proud?"
"That secret in my sick soul fastened
To no man I will tell aloud!

For so long have I been sealing
That same secret in my heart
Not unto the world unfeeling
Will I bare my secret dark:

Not if gold were put before me,
Not for silver, not for fame,
Not if swords were waving o'er me,
Not amid the bonfire's flame!"

Thus he spoke, himself betaking
To the hillside, all in snow.
Now his steed with fear is shaking,
Stumbling onward he does go.

The wayfarer, wrathful, hurries
But his falling steed doth tire,
He no longer favor curries,
Drops his rider in the flurries,
In a snowdrift cold he buries
First himself and then his squire.

He, who thus his secret saved,
Lies buried in a snowy shroud.
He remains beyond the grave
Just as mute and just as proud.

The mysterious Germanic knight is thus transported to the Russian steppe and perishes in a snowdrift. "The Wayfarer" probably parodies a poem published in 1845, "Ezdok",[49] but even here the poet has not dared place his ill-fated rider in Russia itself. Prutkov's poem is a kind of interview, and by making the wayfarer speak aloud, he deprived him of his mute dignity. The most obstinate German knight may keep his secret to the grave; but Prutkov's knight hyperbolically keeps his even beyond it.

A poem which stands in the highest ranks of Prutkovian invention, "The Siege of Pamba" ("Osada Pamby"), is his greatest variation on the theme of the *idée fixe*. In it, not just one knight but a whole besieging army keeps a vow made not to eat any food, but to drink only milk. Thus the absurd is reproduced on an epic scale, and the fifty-one lines of unrhymed trochaic tetrameter give an approximative literary parody of the meter of both the Spanish and the Slavic epic. The poem is subtitled "a romancero[50] from the Spanish", but it shows that its authors, Aleksej Tolstoj and Aleksej Žemčužnikov, were especially well attuned to the cadences of the Slavic epic.

[49] *Ibid.*, p. 436.
[50] *Sic.* The Spanish *romancero* is actually a collection of *romances*.

Девять лет дон Педро Гомец,
По прозванью Лев Кастильи,
Осаждает замок Памбу,
Молоком одним питаясь.
И всё войско дона Педра,
Девять тысяч кастильянцев,
Все, по данному обету,
Не касаются мясного,
Ниже хлеба не снедают,
Пьют одно лишь молоко.
Всякий день они слабеют,
Силы тратя по-пустому.
Всякий день дон Педро Гомец
О своем бессильи плачет,
Закрываясь епанчею.
Настает уж год десятый.
Злые мавры торжествуют;
А от войска дона Педра
Налицо едва осталось
Девятнадцать человек.
Их собрал дон Педро Гомец
И сказал им: «Девятнадцать!
Разовьем свои знамена,
В трубы громкие взыграем
И, ударивши в литавры,
Прочь от Памбы мы отступим,
Без стыда и без боязни.
Хоть мы крепости не взяли,
Но поклясться можем смело
Перед совестью и честью:
Не нарушили ни разу
Нами данного обета, —
Целых девять лет не ели,
Ничего не ели ровно,
Кроме только молока!»
Ободренные сей речью,
Девятнадцать кастильянцев,
Все, качаяся на седлах,
В голос слабо закричали:
Sancto Jago Compostello!
Честь и слава дону Педру,
Честь и слава Льву Кастильи!»
А каплан его Диего
Так сказал себе сквозь зубы:
«Если б я был полководцем,
Я б обет дал есть лишь мясо,
Запивая сантуринским».
И, услышав то, дон Педро

Произнес со громким смехом:
«Подарить ему барана:
Он изрядно подшутил».

For nine years Don Pedro Gomez,
Called the Lion of Castillo,
Has besieged the castle Pamba,
On naught else but milk surviving.
And the army of Don Pedro,
Full nine thousand brave Castilians
Keeping to a promise given
Do not touch a bite of good meat
Nor do they partake of good bread;
All of them drink only milk.
Every day they're growing weaker,
Losing all their strength for nothing.
Every day Don Pedro Gomez
Weeps about his growing weakness,
Folding up his cloak about him.
Now the tenth year is beginning.
Evil Moors begin to triumph;
But from all Don Pedro's army
There are present and remaining
Only nineteen living men.
So Don Pedro Gomez took them
And he told them: "O ye nineteen!
Let us now unfurl our standards,
Let us sound the trumpets loudly
And, with beating of our snare-drums
We will march away from Pamba
Without shame and without fearing.
Though we failed to take the fortress,
Still we may most boldly swear now
On our honor and our conscience
That not once were we renouncing
That great vow which we have taken. —
Nine full years we have not eaten
Eaten absolutely nothing,
Only milk have we been drinking!"
Taking courage at his speech then
All the nineteen brave Castilians
Shaking, swaying in their saddles,
With one voice they called out weakly:
"Sancto Iago Compostello!
Honor, glory to Don Pedro,
Hail the Lion of Castillo!"
But his chaplain named Diego
Muttered to himself with teeth clenched:

"If I were the army's leader,
I would swear to eat meat only,
Drinking it down with santorin."
Overhearing him, Don Pedro
Said these words while laughing loudly:
"Give this man a side of mutton;
Very prettily he banters."

The poem is structured like a miniature epic: first, twenty lines of exposition give the background of the drama (the first ten describe the caprice of Don Pedro, the second ten its result); the next fifteen lines contain Don Pedro's speech which will serve as the catalyst for the present action; and in the final sixteen, the immediate drama unfolds. After this immense build-up, however, the poem ends with a mere snatch of dialogue. Buxštab points out that the last line, with its absurd *noblesse oblige*, echoes a line from P. A. Katenin's translation of "The Romance of the Cid".[51] Such translations and loose imitations of Spanish romances were immensely popular in all of Europe since Herder's translation of 1801, and "The Siege of Pamba" mocks the whole pseudo-epic with its slowly-unfolding plot set around some struggle long past. The humor of the poem derives from small touches as well as large: the use of such verbal archaisms as snedat' and such conceptual archaisms as the notion of honor in keeping a vow until death. As usual, Prutkov treats foreign words capriciously, declining foreign names (Don Pedro, Pamba) but the main formal source of humor is to be found in the insistent repetitions, mainstays of the epic but here lending a cumulatively comic tone to the poem. The magical numbers nine and nineteen, the diet of milk only, the formulas of honor and glory, the long names which fill out lines and all the other repeated words and phrases, normal in the oral epic, assume a humorous function in "The Siege of Pamba". In oral poetry these repetitions have a structural, mnemotechnic and incantatory role, but here the incongruity of the action and the language employed to describe it result in a comic chipping-away of the edifice even as it is being built up.

Oddly enough, "The Siege of Pamba" enjoyed a limited oral success and then re-entered Russian literature. Dostoevskij used the poem in his short novel of 1859, *The Village of Stepančikovo*. He quotes it incorrectly, which proves he must have known it by heart. One character calls it an "innocent, noble satire, harming no one",[52] but in the works of

---

[51] Koz'ma Prutkov, p. 432.
[52] F. M. Dostoevskij, *Sobranie sočinenij*, II, 590.

Dostoevskij nothing is ever completely harmless, and the innocent poem touches off a melodramatic event.

Still, Dostoevskij's character was right. The poetry of Prutkov is basically "innocent and noble, harming no one". The obsessions and extravagance of his characters are self-generating like those of Dostoevskij's characters, but unlike the latter they end right where they began—in the character himself. The innocent humor of the entire work is based upon the guiltlessness of the comic figure of Prutkov himself, which we have analyzed in the previous chapter. And, in an even larger sense, the innocence of Prutkov depends on the motives of his "mentors", whose parodic realizations of certain poetic themes wafting in the mid-nineteenth century air were never meant to harm the poets who used them, if indeed they were still alive.

If "My Portrait" opens the poetic section of Prutkov's works with a romantic gesture of defiance, the poem his editors place last, "Before Death" ("Predsmertnoe"), is a final gesture of comic innocence:

Вот час последних сил упадка
От органических причин. . .
Прости, Пробирная палатка,
Где я снискал высокий чин,
Но музы не отверг объятий
Среди мне вверенных занятий!

Мне до могилы два-три шага. . .
Прости мой стих! и ты, перо!
И ты, о писчая бумага,
На коей сеял я добро!
Уж я — потухшая лампадка
Иль опрокинутая лодка!

Вот. . . все пришли. . . Друзья, бог помочь!. . .
Стоят гишпанцы, греки вкруг. . .
Вот юнкер Шмидт. . . Принес Пахомыч
На гроб мне незабудок пук. . .
Зовет Кондуктор. . . Ах!. .

Now the last strength ebbs away
Due to causes organic...
Farewell now, Office of Assay
Where I held highest rank,
But never spurned the muse's embrace
Despite my highly trusted place!

I have to grave's edge but a caper...
Farewell, my verse! and you, my quill!
To you, farewell, oh writing paper
On which I sowed naught but good-will!
Already I'm a lamp out-burned
Or else a rowboat overturned.

Now all have come... My friends, God save!
There stand the Spaniards, Greeks in throng
Here's Junker Schmidt... Paxomyč to the grave
Brough some forget-me-nots along...
The driver calls... Ah!...

The poem and its accompanying "Indispensable explanation" were written by Vladimir Žemčužnikov. The latter describes how Prutkov dies in
the middle of the poem, leaving a large inkblot on the manuscript.
It was written in the Office of Assay, and contains a dual farewell—to
government and to literary service. It gives a quintessential demonstration
of the Prutkovian style—an extremely adept mixture of ineptitudes: the
prosaic diction of the second line following the involuted syntax of the
first; the rhetorical farewells to things imaginary and real; the metaphor
of the muse's embrace made concrete by its location in a real office setting; the mixing of metaphor (sowing good on writing paper); the search
for metaphor within the poem itself in the last two lines of the second
stanza (the idea being that two metaphors are always better than one).
At the end, the characters recalled seem to step out of their poems and
take on life. The driver becomes a kind of Charon, ready to lead Prutkov
into the other world. Thus Prutkov tried to immortalize even his own
death in verse, but left the world an incomplete rhyme. Perhaps even
this ending was totally conscious and planned like the rest of Prutkov's
art.

The Žemčužnikovs and Tolstoj created a character self-obsessed and
poetically obsessed who in turn created other obsessed and poetically
exaggerated characters in a parody of the creative process. But in spite
of seeming anti-creative, anti-spontaneous and anti-intuitive, Prutkov's
art is none of these. The peculiar Prutkovian handling of metaphors, the
rhetorical repetitions, the beloved vocabulary with its prosaic poeticisms
—all the often-repeated stylistic devices are not the essence of Prutkov.
In a poem called "Ambition" ("Čestoljubie") when Prutkov calls upon
some unknown power to give him the strength of Samson, the mind of
Socrates and the attributes of a dozen of the more famous ancients, he
includes a request for a magic wand in the catalogue. This may indicate

Prutkovian prudence; just in case classical references fail to do the job, something better should be held in reserve. But it may also be taken as a metaphor for Prutkov's real artistic success. Prutkov uses devices of romanticism or classical references with such insistent overemphasis; but ultimately he believes not in these outworn styles but in the magic of true literary creativity. This belief channels the destructive force of parody into a creative new style. The grab-bag of outworn devices is magically revitalized by the figure of the poet-bureaucrat who employs them.

The poet's biography has always been a source of passionate interest to readers of poetry, and even the present generation has not been entirely weaned from it by the new criticism, which has substituted nothing better. Prutkov creates other characters, but he is always the hero of his poems, and this fact is a source of ultimate satisfaction to his reader. To be told in plain terms that Prutkov is married and has a large number of children is not as good as reading a poem about his marriage:

К ДРУЗЬЯМ ПОСЛЕ ЖЕНИТЬБЫ

Я женился; небо вняло
Нашим пламенным мольбам;
Сердце сердцу весть подало,
Страсть ввела нас в светлый храм.

О друзья! ваш страх напрасен,
У меня ль не твердый нрав?
В гневе я суров, ужасен,
Страж лихой супружних прав.

Есть для мести черным ковам
У женатого певца
Над кроватью, под альковом,
Нож, ружье и фунт свинца!

Нож вострей швейцарской бритвы;
Пули меткие в мешке;
А ружье на поле битвы
Я нашел в сыром песке..

Тем ружьем в былое время
По драхвам певец стрелял
И, клянусь, всегда им в темя
Всем зарядом попадал!

TO MY FRIENDS, AFTER MARRIAGE

I got married; heaven harkened
To our burning lovers' prayer;
Heart gave out the news to heart and
Passion oped her temple fair.

Oh my friends! You need not fear
Do you think my mores light?
Awesome in my wrath, severe,
I'll guard well my married rights.

Black perfidy requires revenge.
So in the alcove, o'er the bed,
The married poet has arranged
A knife, a gun, a pound of lead!

The knife is sharper than Swiss steel;
The bag of bullets near at hand;
The rifle's from a battle-field,
I found it in the damp, wet sand...

With this gun in times gone by
The poet shot the bustards down;
I swear that with a full supply
He always hit them in the crown.

Prutkov, in this poem, is daydreaming himself into a romantic situation. He has married, the first words tell us. But the rest is imagination. His passion has been sanctified, but woe to the passions of others, for he has turned the marriage chamber into a veritable arsenal. We are not in the Caucasus or among the gypsies, but in a Russian city. Prutkov has used that magic wand which enables him to create romantic poetry in unlikely places.

The poem bears all the Prutkovian trademarks. It is written in a traditional genre—here the epistle. It is written in Prutkov's favorite quatrains of trochaic tetrameter with cross-rhymes. It takes a situation, exaggerates it, and contrasts it with reality. The romantic images bear small but deadly seeds of their own destruction: the gun found in damp sand would probably be rusty; and the very combination of the words "ženatyj pevec" is, somehow, absurd. The poem parodies some lines of Benediktov;[53] but, like most of Prutkov's poetry, it is felt not as parody of a few

---

[53] Koz'ma Prutkov, pp. 39-40.

lines nor even of one poet. It parodies the ever-present urge to romanticize in life and in literature. It gives the reader the triple satisfaction of
relishing a romantic situation, destroying it himself without any emotional
agony by reading the verses, and keeping the short, perfect poem as a
souvenir of the whole venture.

CONCLUSION

As parody, the works of Koz'ma Prutkov tend more towards humor than polemics. In the case of Prutkov, we reject the notion of parody being literary criticism or part of a literary struggle. When Prutkov's mentors wrote in genres ripe for doom, they did not intend to annihilate the genre, but to use it as a container for humor. Formally, the result of this parodic writing was not a criticism of an author's work, but a humorous revamping of it. Historically, Prutkov's poetry did not serve as a force of literary change.

The purpose of this work has been to describe the literary phenomenon of Koz'ma Prutkov both in its inception and in its realization. Prutkov arose from the individual and collective reactions of several nineteenth-century Russians to bureaucratic life and to art. Their sense of the absurd in various poems and poetic traditions provided the impetus to write humorous poetry, which often took the form of parody. The parody in turn served as the spring-board,[1] the stylistic point of departure, for a unique body of writing, so diverse, in spite of its stylistic repetitions, that only the created figure of its author gives it unity. Nearly every separate work of Prutkov's has a separate inspiration and each realization is somewhat different. Each work is brief, compressing a whole tradition and sometimes a whole era in a few lines or pages. Parody cannot be too brief (its annals contain works of one line), and it risks losing its effect if it is too long.

Tynjanov distinguishes between *parodijnost'* (the state of being parody) and *parodičnost'* (the state of containing elements of parody), but then blurs the distinction by saying that "both phenomena are close to each other and usually coexist".[2] Morozov somewhat less skillfully makes

[1] Tynjanov says that parody can be merely the spring-board (tramplin) to introduce topical material into literature. (Ju. N. Tynjanov, *Mnimaja poezija*, p. 8). This function really subordinates the parodic element to the satiric one. We are using the spring-board image in a different sense: the urge to parody produces literature that is not always ultimately parodic.
[2] *Ibid.*

much the same distinction between general parody *(parodijnost')* and the parody of separate literary phenomena *(parodirovanie)*.[3] As we have seen, Prutkov's works, taken individually, when they are not parody *per se*, nearly always contain elements of parody.

In the largest and most general sense, however, the works of Koz'ma Prutkov are a parody of the conscious creation of literature. Northrop Frye writes of doggerel:

> It has a prose initiative, but tries to make itself associative by an act of will, and it reveals the same difficulties that great poetry has overcome at a subconscious level. We can see in doggerel how words are dragged in because they are suggested by a rhyme-word, and so on. Deliberate doggerel ... can be a source of brilliant rhetorical satire, and one which involves a kind of parody of poetic creation itself...[4]

Prutkov's writings are premeditated art—the striking of a romantic pose, the conscious writing of a vaudeville, the careful editing of historical materials, or the exquisite fashioning of an aphorism. They are inspired parody of uninspired art.

In introducing Koz'ma Prutkov, we spoke of his immense popularity practically since his first appearance; by contrast, Prutkov has had little impact on the course of Russian literature. It would be hard to demonstrate that Prutkov's work was "one of the elements of the dialectic change of schools", to use Tynjanov's phrase.[5] It would even be difficult to point to an immediate influence on a particular author. Dostoevskij may have used the same kind of absurd characters and unmotivated situations as Prutkov, but they were his own, and he always subordinated comedy to a larger psychological and metaphysical drama. Still, he recognized Prutkov as a kindred spirit.

Jorge Luis Borges writes brilliantly about the real nature of an influence—how a particular author alters the perception of literature not just in the present but in the past as well:

> In the critics' vocabulary, the word "precursor" is indispensable, but it should be cleansed of all connotation of polemics or rivalry. The fact is that every writer *creates* his own precursors. His work modifies our conception of the past, as it will modify the future. In this correlation, the identity or plurality of the men involved is unimportant.[6]

---

[3] A. A. Morozov, "Parodija kak literaturnyj žanr (k teorii parodii)", p. 52.
[4] Northrop Frye, *Anatomy of Criticism* (New York: Atheneum, 1966), p. 277.
[5] Ju. N. Tynjanov, "Dostoevskij i Gogol' (k teorii parodii)", *Arxaisty i Novatory*, p. 433.
[6] Jorge Luis Borges, *Labyrinths* (New York: New Directions, 1962), p. 201.

Thus, demons of medieval Russian literature suddenly become Gogolian, scenes from Stendhal deepen in meaning because of Tolstoj, and we see too much human psychology in Gogol' because of Dostoevskij. Benediktov and the Slavophiles are doomed to be seen through Prutkovian eyes, as is Gumilev when he seemingly inadvertently writes such a poem as "The Old Conquistador".[7]

The romantic tradition was variously transformed by the Russians of the nineteenth century, and the greatest writers were the greatest transformers. Puškin, Gogol', Tolstoj and Dostoevskij all struggled with one or more of the demons of romanticism, and in conquering, each created his unique style. Koz'ma Prutkov, that bureaucrat with romantic impulses and a prosaic mind, conquered the easy way—by parody and humor—but the victory is as complete and the literary result as unique.

---

[7]   N. S. Gumilev, *Sobranie sočinenij* (Washington: Victor Kamkin Inc., 1962), I, 108.

APPENDIX

TWENTY TRANSLATIONS FROM KOZ'MA PRUTKOV

МОЙ ПОРТРЕТ

Когда в толпе ты встретишь человека,
    Который наг;[1]
Чей лоб мрачней туманного Казбека,
    Неровен шаг;
Кого власы подъяты в беспорядке;
    Кто, вопия,
Всегда дрожит в нервическом припадке, —
    Знай: это я!

Когда язвят, со злостью вечно новой,
    Из рода в род;
С кого толпа венец его лавровый
    Безумно рвет;
Кто ни пред кем спины не клонит гибкой, —
    Знай: это я!. .
В моих устах спокойная улыбка,
    В груди — змея!

MY PORTRAIT

When in the crowd you meet a man somehow
    Who naked goes;[2]
Gloomier than the fogged Kazbek his brow,
    Unsure he roves;
Whose tresses rumple up in disarray;
    Who, with a cry,
Forever trembles in a nervous way,—
    Know: it is I!

Whom people taunt in ever-growing quarrel,
    Throughout the years;

[1] *Вариапт:* «На коем фрак». *Примечание К. Пруткоба.*
[2] *Variant:* "Who's wearing clothes." Note by K. Prutkov.

From whom the madding throng his wreath of laurel
   In folly tears;
Who before no man bends his knee so supple,—
   Know: it is I!
Upon my lips there plays a smile untroubled,
   In my breast—serpents lie!

НЕЗАБУДКИ И ЗАПЯТКИ
БАСНЯ

Трясясь Пахомыч на запятках,
Пук незабудок вез с собой;
Мозоли натерев на пятках,
Лечил их дома камфарой.

Читатель! в басне сей откинув незабудки,
   Здесь помещенные для шутки,
   Ты только это заключи:
   Коль будут у тебя мозоли,
   То, чтоб избавиться от боли,
Ты, как Пахомыч наш, их камфарой лечи.

FORGET-ME-NOTS AND FOOTBOARDS
A FABLE

Paxomyč, bumping on the wheels,
Took some forget-me-nots along;
Acquiring bunions on his heels,
He treated them with camphor strong.

Pray, drop the flowers of which we spoke,
   They're only added for a joke,
   This problem has one answer:
   If your bunions hurt again,
   In order to relieve the pain,
Like our Paxomyč, pamper them with camphor.

КОНДУКТОР И ТАРАНТУЛ
БАСНЯ

В горах Гишпании тяжелый экипаж
   С кондуктором отправился в вояж.
   Гишпанка, севши в нем, немедленно заснула.
   А муж ее меж тем, увидя таранту́ла,
      Вскричал: «Кондуктор, стой!
   Приди скорей! Ах, боже мой!»
   На крик кондуктор поспешает

И тут же веником скотину выгоняет,
Примолвив: «Денег ты за место не платил!»
И тотчас же его пятою раздавил.
Читатель! разочти вперед свои депансы,
Чтоб даром не дерзать садиться в дилижансы,
И норови, чтобы отнюдь
Без денег не пускаться в путь;
Не то случится и с тобой, что с насекомым,
Тебе знакомым.

THE DRIVER AND THE TARANTULA

A FABLE

In the Spanish mountains a heavy équipage
With a driver set out en voyage.
A Spanish lady slept inside. Her
Husband, meanwhile, glimpsed a giant spider
And cried, "Oh, driver, wait!
Come quickly; it may be too late!"
The driver hurried at the shout,
And with a broom swept the beast out.
He said, "You haven't bought a ticket!"
And with his heel began to kick it.

Friend! Calculate ahead all your expenses;
Do not sit down in vain in diligences.
But follow, please, this precedent:
Do not set forth without a cent.
Unless you seek the fate of that same pet
Whom you have met.

ЮНКЕР ШМИДТ

Вянет лист. Проходит лето.
Иней серебрится. . .
Юнкер Шмидт из пистолета
Хочет застрелиться.

Погоди, безумный, снова
Зелень оживится!
Юнкер Шмидт! честно́е слово,
Лето возвратится!

JUNKER SCHMIDT

Fades the leaf. The Summer's over.
Hoar-frost starts to fall...

Junker Schmidt, with a revolver
Wants to end it all.

Wait, oh madman, somewhere yonder
Green you will discern!
Junker Schmidt, my word of honor,
Summer will return!

ЭПИГРАММА
№I

«Вы любите ли сыр?» — спросили раз ханжу.
«Люблю, — он отвечал, — я вкус в нем нахожу».

EPIGRAM No. I

"And are you fond of cheese"—they asked the bigot once.
"I am"—he answered them—"It's rather nice to munch."

ПАМЯТЬ ПРОШЛОГО
КАК БУДТО ИЗ ГЕЙНЕ

Помню я тебя ребенком,
Скоро будет сорок лет;
Твой передничек измятый,
Твой затянутый корсет.

Было в нем тебе неловко;
Ты сказала мне тайком:
«Распусти корсет мне сзади;
Не могу я бегать в нем».

Весь исполненный волненья,
Я корсет твой развязал. . .
Ты со смехом убежала,
Я ж задумчиво стоял.

A MEMORY OF BYGONE DAYS
AS THOUGH FROM HEINE

I remember you in childhood,
Almost forty years ago;
With your rumpled pinafore on,
With your corset laced in so.

In it you were feeling awkward;
And you told me secretly:
"Let my corset out in back now;
In it I cannot run free."

All suffused with agitation,
I your corset then unwound...
You ran off with happy laughter,
I stood still in thought profound.

ДРЕВНИЙ ПЛАСТИЧЕСКИЙ ГРЕК

Люблю тебя, дева, когда золотистый
И солнцем облитый ты держишь лимон,
И юноши зрю подбородок пушистый
Меж листьев аканфа и белых колонн.

Красивой хламиды тяжелые складки
    Упали одна за другой...
Так в улье шумящем, вкруг раненой матки,
    Снует озабоченный рой.

THE ANCIENT PLASTIC GREEK

I love you, my sweet girl, whenever you're holding
A fine golden lemon, all drenched in the light,
The soft downy chin of a youth I'm beholding
Twixt leaves of acantha and columns of white.

The loose, heavy pleats of the beautiful chlamys
    One after the other fell free...
And thus in the beehive around their hurt queen press
    The swarms of solicitous bees.

В АЛЬБОМ КРАСИВОЙ ЧУЖЕСТРАНКЕ
НАПИСАНО В МОСКВЕ

Вокруг тебя очарованье.
Ты бесподобна. Ты мила.
Ты силой чудной обаянья
К себе поэта привлекла.
Но он любить тебя не может:
Ты родилась в чужом краю,
И он охулки не положит,
Любя тебя, на честь свою.

IN THE ALBUM OF A BEAUTIFUL FOREIGNER

WRITTEN IN MOSCOW

Around you an enchanted bower.
You are unequalled. You are sweet.
By wond'rous fascinating power
You've brought the poet to your feet.
But from your love he must refrain:
For you were born abroad somewhere,
And he's no dope to go and stain,
By loving you, his honor fair.

ОСАДА ПАМБЫ

РОМАНСЕРО, С ИСПАНСКОГО

Девять лет дон Педро Гомец,
По прозванью Лев Кастильи,
Осаждает замок Памбу,
Молоком одним питаясь.
И всё войско дона Педра,
Девять тысяч кастильянцев,
Все, по данному обету,
Не касаются мясного,
Ниже хлеба не снедают,
Пьют одно лишь молоко.
Всякий день они слабеют,
Силы тратя по-пустому.
Всякий день дон Педро Гомец
О своем бессильи плачет,
Закрываясь епанчею.
Настает уж год десятый.
Злые мавры торжествуют;
А от войска дона Педра
Налицо едва осталось
Девятнадцать человек.
Их собрал дон Педро Гомец
И сказал им: «Девятнадцать!
Разовьем свои знамена,
В трубы громкие взыграем
И, ударивши в литавры,
Прочь от Памбы мы отступим,
Без стыда и без боязни.
Хоть мы крепости не взяли,
Но поклясться можем смело
Перед совестью и честью:
Не нарушили ни разу

Нами данного обета, —
Целых девять лет не ели,
Ничего не ели ровно,
Кроме только молока!»
Ободренные сей речью,
Девятнадцать кастильянцев,
Все, качаяся на седлах,
В голос слабо закричали:
„Sancto Jago Compostello!¹
Честь и слава дону Педру,
Честь и слава Льву Кастильи»!
А каплан его Диего
Так сказал себе сквозь зубы:
«Если б я был полководцем,
Я б обет дал есть лишь мясо,
Запивая сантуринским».
И, услышав то, дон Педро
Произнес со громким смехом:
«Подарить ему барана:
Он изрядно подшутил».

THE SIEGE OF PAMBA
A ROMANCERO, FROM THE SPANISH

For nine years Don Pedro Gomez,
Called the Lion of Castillo,
Has besieged the castle Pamba,
On naught else but milk surviving.
And the army of Don Pedro,
Full nine thousand brave Castilians
Keeping to a promise given
Do not touch a bite of good meat
Nor do they partake of good bread;
All of them drink only milk.
Every day they're growing weaker,
Losing all their strength for nothing.
Every day Don Pedro Gomez
Weeps about his growing weakness,
Folding up his cloak about him.
Now the tenth year is beginning.
Evil Moors begin to triumph;
But from all Don Pedro's army
There are present and remaining
Only nineteen living men.
So Don Pedro Gomez took them
And he told them: "O ye nineteen!
Let us now unfurl our standards,

Let us sound the trumpets loudly
And, with beating of our snare-drums,
We will march away from Pamba
Without shame and without fearing.
Though we failed to take the fortress,
Still we may most boldly swear now
On our honor and our conscience
That not once were we renouncing
That great vow which we have taken,—
Nine full years we have not eaten
Eaten absolutely nothing,
Only milk have we been drinking!"
Taking courage at his speech then
All the nineteen brave Castilians
Shaking, swaying in their saddles,
With one voice they called out weakly:
"Sancto Iago Compostello!
Hail the Lion of Castillo!"
But his chaplain named Diego
Muttered to himself with teeth clenched:
"If I were the army's leader,
I would swear to eat meat only,
Drinking it down with santorin."
Overhearing him, Don Pedro
Said these words while laughing loudly:
"Give this man a side of mutton;
Very prettily he banters."

ЭПИГРАММА
№ II

Мне, в размышлении глубоком,
Сказал однажды Лизимах:
«Что зрячий зрит здоровым оком,
Слепой не видит и в очках!»

EPIGRAM No. II

In profoundest meditation
Lysimachus said one time:
"The seeing see with healthy vision,
The blind with glasses still are blind."

НА ВЗМОРЬЕ

На взморье, у самой заставы,
Я видел большой огород.
Растет там высокая спаржа;
Капуста там скромно растет.

Там утром всегда огородник
Лениво проходит меж гряд;
На нем неопрятный передник;
Угрюм его пасмурный взгляд.

Польет он из лейки капусту;
Он спаржу небрежно польет;
Нарежет зеленого луку
И после глубоко вздохнет.

Намедни к нему подъезжает
Чиновник на тройке лихой.
Он в теплых, высоких галошах;
На шее лорнет золотой.

«Где дочка твоя?» — вопрошает
Чиновник, прищурясь в лорнет.
Но, дико взглянув, огородник
Махнул лишь рукою в ответ.

И тройка назад поскакала,
Сметая с капусты росу ..
Стоит огородник угрюмо
И пальцем копает в носу.

AT THE SEASHORE

Right up at the gates by the seashore
I saw a large garden below.
The lofty asparagus grows there;
There cabbages modestly grow.

And there every morning the gardener
Goes lazily round twixt the beds;
And wearing a messy old apron;
Looks sullen and gloomy ahead.

He waters a pot on the cabbage;
And on the asparagus dry;
He cuts off the green of the onion
And afterwards heaves a deep sigh.

But lately to him in a troika
Comes riding a bureaucrat bold.
All dressed up in warm high galoshes,
And wearing a lorgnette of gold.

"Oh, where is your daughter?"—so questions
The bureaucrat, scrunching his eyes,
But, looking quite savage, the gardener
Just flung out his arm in reply.

And backwards the troika it gallops,
The dew from the cabbage it blows...
The gardener stands looking sullen
And silently picking his nose.

НОВОГРЕЧЕСКАЯ ПЕСНЬ

Спит залив. Эллада дремлет.
Под портик уходит мать
Сок гранаты выжимать...
Зоя! нам никто не внемлет!
Зоя, дай себя обнять!

Зоя, утренней порою
Я уйду отсюда прочь;
Ты смягчись, покуда ночь!
Зоя, утренней порою
Я уйду отсюда прочь...

Пусть же вихрем сабля свищет!
Мне Костаки не судья!
Прав Костаки, прав и я!
Пусть же вихрем сабля свищет;
Мне Костаки не судья!

В поле брани Разорваки
Пал за вольность как герой.
Бог с ним! рок его такой.
Но зачем же жив Костаки,
Когда в поле Разорваки
Пал за вольность как герой?!

Видел я вчера в заливе
Восемнадцать кораблей;
Все без мачт и без рулей...
Но султана я счастливей;
Лей вина мне, Зоя, лей!

Лей, пока Эллада дремлет,
Пока тщетно тщится мать
Сок гранаты выжимать...
Зоя, нам никто не внемлет!
Зоя, дай себя обнять!

A MODERN GREEK SONG

The gulf is sleeping. Hellas drowses.
Through porticoes your mother leaves
Pomegranate juice to squeeze...
Zoya! Not a soul it rouses!
Zoya! Come, embrace me, please!

Zoya, I from here must hasten
E'en before the night is spent;
While it's dark yet, please relent!
Zoya, I from here must hasten
E'en before the night is spent...

May my sword swish like a whirlwind!
Kostaki is no judge of me!
I am right and so is he!
May my sword swish like a whirlwind;
Kostaki is no judge of me!

In the battle Razorvaki
Fell, a hero for free Greece.
That's his fate; God grant him peace.
But why is he alive, Kostaki,
When in battle Razorvaki
Fell, a hero for free Greece?!

Yesterday in the gulf waters
Eighteen ships there did appear;
None had masts nor helms to steer...
I'm happier still than a vizir;
Pour the wine out, Zoya, dear!

Pour while all of Hellas drowses
Agreeably, mother now agrees
Pomegranate juice to squeeze...
Zoya, not a soul it rouses!
Zoya, come, embrace me, please!

В АЛЬБОМ N. N.

Желанья вашего всегда покорный раб,
Из книги дней моих я вырву полстраницы
И в ваш альбом вклею... Вы знаете, я слаб
Пред волей женщины, тем более девицы.
Вклею!.. Но вижу я, уж вас объемлет страх!
Змеей тоски моей пришлось мне поделиться;
Не целая змея теперь во мне, но — ах! —
Зато по ползмеи в обоих шевелится.

IN THE ALBUM OF N. N.

Ever your humble servant when you speak,
Out of my diary half a page I tear
And paste it in your book... You know I'm weak
Before the will of woman, the more so maiden fair.
I paste it in!... But now you tremble so!
Of my heart's serpent now you do partake;
Now not one serpent lies in me, but—oh!—
In each of us there wriggles half a snake.

ОСЕНЬ
С ПЕРСИДСКОГО, ИЗ ИБН-ФЕТА

Осень. Скучно. Ветер воет.
Мелкий дождь по окнам льет.
Ум тоскует; сердце ноет;
И душа чего-то ждет.

И в бездейственном покое
Нечем скуку мне отвест...
Я не знаю: что такое?
Хоть бы книжку мне прочесть!

AUTUMN
(FROM THE PERSIAN, AFTER IBN-FET)

Autumn. Boredom. Wind is wailing.
Small rain patters on the pane.
Mind is anguished; heart is ailing;
Soul awaits something in vain.
In my comfortable inertia
Boredom looms where'er I look.
I don't know, what is the matter?
Wish that I could read a book!

ПУТНИК
БАЛЛАДА

Путник едет косогором;
Путник по полю спешит.
Он обводит тусклым взором
Степи снежной грустный вид.

«Ты к кому спешишь на встречу,
Путник гордый и немой?»
— «Никому я не отвечу:
Тайна то души больной!

Уж давно я тайну эту
Хороню в груди своей,
И бесчувственному свету
Не открою тайны сей:

Ни за знатность, ни за злато,
Ни за груды серебра,
Ни под взмахами булата,
Ни средь пламени костра!»

Он сказал — и вдаль несется
Косогором, весь в снегу.
Конь испуганный трясется,
Спотыкаясь на бегу.

Путник с гневом погоняет
Карабагского коня.
Конь усталый упадает,
Седока с собой роняет
И под снегом погребает
Господина и себя.

Схороненный под сугробом,
Путник тайну скрыл с собой.
Он пребудет и за гробом
Тот же гордый и немой.

THE WAYFARER
A BALLAD

The wayfarer rides o'er the hill;
Now he hastens through the fields;
Round he looks with glances dull
At the steppe in snow congealed.

"To what meeting do you hasten,
O wayfarer mute and proud?"
"That secret in my sick soul fastened;
To no man I will tell aloud!

For so long have I been sealing
That same secret in my heart
Not unto the world unfeeling
Will I bare that secret dark:

Not if gold were put before me,
Not for silver, not for fame,
Not if swords were waving o'er me,
Not amid the bonfire's flame!"

Thus he spoke, himself betaking
To the hillside all in snow.
Now his steed with fear is shaking,
Stumbling onward he doth go.

The wayfarer, wrathful, hurries
But his falling steed doth tire,
He no longer favor curries,
Drops his rider in the flurries,
In a snowdrift cold he buries
First himself and then his squire.

He, who thus his secret saved,
Lies buried in a snowy shroud.
He remains beyond the grave
Just as mute and just as proud.

ПАСТУХ, МОЛОКО И ЧИТАТЕЛЬ
БАСНЯ

Однажды нес пастух куда-то молоко.
　　　　　Но так ужасно далеко,
　　　　　Что уж назад не возвращался.

Читатель! он тебе не попадался?

THE COWHERD, THE MILK,
AND THE READER
A FABLE

Once a cowherd took some milk,
　　　　But he went so far astray
　　　　That he never did return.
Reader, has he passed your way?

ЭПИГРАММА
№ III

Пия душистый сок цветочка,
Пчела дает нам мед взамен;
Хотя твой лоб пустая бочка,
Но всё же ты не Диоген.

EPIGRAM No. III

Drinking the fragrant flower's their task;
We get our honey from the bees;
Although your head's an empty cask,
You still are no Diogenes.

ПЯТКИ НЕКСТАТИ
БАСНЯ

У кого болит затылок,
Тот уж пяток не чеши!
Мой сосед был слишком пылок
(Жил в деревне он, в глуши):
Раз случись ему, гуляя,
Головой задеть сучок;
Он, недолго размышляя,
Осердяся на толчок,
Хвать рукой за обе пятки —
И затем в грязь носом хвать!

Многие привычки гадки,
Но скверней не отыскать
Пятки попусту чесать!

HEELS INAPPROPRIATE
A FABLE

If it itches on your head,
Don't begin to scratch your heels!
My neighbor was by passion led.
He lived in country, in the fields.
Once this man, as he went walking,
Brushed his head against a tree;
Considered it and, hardly balking,

Took the bump quite angrily,
Grabbed both heels and with a thud—
Took a nose-dive in the mud!...

There are many vicious habits,
But no nastier may be sought
As than to scratch one's heels for naught!

К ДРУЗЬЯМ ПОСЛЕ ЖЕНИТЬБЫ

Я женился; небо вняло
Нашим пламенным мольбам;
Сердце сердцу весть подало,
Страсть ввела нас в светлый храм.

О друзья! ваш страх напрасен,
У меня ль не твердый нрав?
В гневе я суров, ужасен,
Страж лихой супружних прав.

Есть для мести черным ковам
У женатого певца
Над кроватью, под альковом,
Нож, ружье и фунт свинца!

Нож вострей швейцарской бритвы;
Пули меткие в мешке;
А ружье на поле битвы
Я нашел в сыром песке...

Тем ружьем в былое время
По драхвам певец стрелял
И, клянусь, всегда им в темя
Всем зарядом попадал!

TO MY FRIENDS, AFTER MARRIAGE

I got married; heaven hearkened
To our burning lovers' prayer;
Heart gave out the news to heart and
Passion oped her temple fair.

Oh my friends! You need not fear
Do you think my mores light?
Awesome in my wrath, severe,
I'll guard well my married rights.

Black perfidy requires revenge.
So in the alcove, o'er the bed,
The married poet has arranged
A knife, a gun, a pound of lead!

The knife is sharper than Swiss steel;
The bag of bullets near at hand;
The rifle's from a battle-field,
I found it in the damp, wet sand...

With this gun in times gone by
The poet shot the bustards down;
I swear that with a full supply
He always hit them in the crown.

ПРЕДСМЕРТНОЕ

НАЙДЕНО НЕДАВНО, ПРИ РЕВИЗИИ ПРОБИРНОЙ ПАЛАТКИ, В ДЕЛАХ СЕЙ ПОСЛЕДНЕЙ

Вот час последних сил упадка
От органических причин...
Прости, Пробирная палатка,
Где я снискал высокий чин,
Но музы не отверг объятий
Среди мне вверенных занятий!

Мне до могилы два-три шага...
Прости, мой стих! и ты, перо!
И ты, о писчая бумага,
На коей сеял я добро!
Уж я — потухшая лампадка
Иль опрокинутая лодка!

Вот... все пришли... Друзья, бог помочь!..
Стоят гишпанцы, греки вкруг...
Вот юнкер Шмидт... Принес Пахомыч
На гроб мне незабудок пук...
Зовет Кондуктор... Ах!..

BEFORE DEATH

FOUND RECENTLY AT THE INSPECTION OF THE OFFICE OF ASSAY IN THE PAPERS OF THE LATTER

Now the last strength ebbs away
Due to causes organic...

Farewell now, Office of Assay
Where I held highest rank,
But never spurned the muse's embrace
Despite my highly trusted place!

I have to grave's edge but a caper...
Farewell, my verse! and you, my quill!
To you, farewell, oh writing paper,
On which I sowed naught but good-will!
Already I'm a lamp out-burned
Or else a rowboat overturned.

Now all have come... My friends, God save!
There stand the Spaniards, Greeks in throng...
Here's Junker Schmidt... Paxomyč to the grave
Brought some forget-me-nots along...
The driver calls... Ah!...

SELECTED BIBLIOGRAPHY

BOOKS

Ajxenval'd, Ju. I. *Siluety russkix pisatelej* (Moscow, 1910). Vol. III.
Amfiteatrov, A. V. *Zabytyj smex*, Vols. I-II (Moscow, 1914).
Athenaeus. *Deiphnosophists* xv.
Batjuškov, K. N. *Sočinenija* (Moscow, 1955).
Benediktov, V. G. *Stixotvorenija* (Leningrad, 1939).
Berkov, P. N. *Koz'ma Prutkov—direktor Probirnoj palatki i poet. K istorii russkoj parodii* (Leningrad–Moscow: Academia Nauk SSSR, 1933).
Borges, Jorge Luis. *Labyrinths* (New York: New Directions, 1962).
Breton, André. *Les manifestes du surréalisme* (Paris: Sagittarius, 1946).
—, *Nadja* (Paris: Gallimard, 1964).
Burke, Kenneth. *The Philosophy of Literary Form* (New York: Random House, 1957).
Buxštab, B. Ta. *Russkie poety* (Leningrad, 1970).
Cammaerts, Emile. *The Poetry of Nonsense* (New York: E. P. Dutton and Company, 1926).
Champfleury. *Henry Monnier, sa vie, son oeuvre* (Paris: E. Dentu, 1879).
Chesterton, G. K. *The Defendant* (New York: Dodd, Mead and Company, 1906).
Dostoevskij, F. M. *Sobranie sočinenij* (Moscow, 1956). Vols. II, IV and VII.
Družinin, A. V. *Polnoe sobranie sočinenij* (Petersburg, 1865). Vol. VI.
Eichrodt, Ludwig. *Lyrische Karrikaturen: eine Anthologie* (Lahr: Verlag Moritz Schauenburg, 1869).
Eliot, T. S. *Selected Essays* (New York: Harcourt, Brace and Company, 1950).
Fet, A. A. *Polnoe sobranie sočinenij* (Leningrad, 1959).
Fordyce, C. J. *Catullus: A Commentary* (Oxford: The Clarendon Press, 1961).
Freud, Sigmund. *Jokes and Their Relation to the Unconscious*, Translated and edited by James Strachey (New York: W. W. Norton and Company, 1963).
Frye, Northrop. *Anatomy of Criticism* (New York: Atheneum, 1966).
Gibian, George (trans. and ed.) *Russia's Lost Literature of The Absurd* (Ithaca: Cornell University Press, 1971).
Grigor'ev, A. A. *Polnoe sobranie sočinenij i pisem* (Petrograd, 1918).
Gumilev, N. S. *Sobranie sočinenij* (Washington: Victor Kamkin, Inc., 1962). Vol. I.
Heine, Heinrich. *Werke und Briefe* (Berlin: Aufbau Verlag, 1961).
Ivanov-Razumnik, P. V. *Istorija russkoj obščestvennoj mysli*, 2d ed. (Petersburg, 1907). Vol. I.
Kovalevskij, E. P. *Sobranie sočinenij*. St. Petersburg, 1871. Vol. I.
Lirondelle, André. *Le poète Alexis Tolstoi, l'homme et l'oeuvre* (Paris: Hachette, 1912).

Locker-Lampson, Frederick (ed.). *Lyra Elegantiarum* (New York: Frederick A. Stokes and Brother, 1889).
Macdonald, Dwight (ed.). *Parodies* (New York: Random House, 1960).
Marmontel, J.-F. *Eléments de littérature* (Paris, 1787).
Monnier, Henri, *Mémoires de monsieur Joseph Prudhomme* (Paris: Librairie Nouvelle, 1857).
Morozov, A. A. (ed.). *Russkaja stixotvornaja parodija* (XVIII-načalo XX veka) (Leningrad, 1960).
Oksman, J. G. (ed.). *Fel'etony sorokovyx godov* (Moscow–Leningrad: Academia, 1930).
Poety 1840-1850-x godov. Edited by B. Ja. Buxštab and V. S. Kiseleva (Moscow–Leningrad, 1962).
Prutkov, Koz'ma. *Polnoe sobranie sočinenij*. Edited by P. N. Berkov (Moscow–Leningrad: Academia, 1933).
—, *Polnoe sobranie sočinenij*. Edited by B. Ja. Buxštab (Moscow–Leningrad, 1965).
—, *Proizvedenija ne vošedšie v sobranie sočinenij*. Edited by P. K. Guber (Petrograd, 1923).
Quintilian. *Institutio Oratoria*, VI.
Rozanov, Ivan. *Literaturnye reputacii* (Moscow, 1928).
Ščerbina, A. A. *Suščnost' i iskusstvo slovesnoj ostroty (kalambura)* (Kiev, 1958).
Sukiasova, I. M. *Jazyk i stil' parodij Koz'my Prutkova; leksiko-stilističeskij analiz* (Tbilisi, 1961).
Tolstoj, A. K. *Sobranie sočinenij* (Moscow, 1964). Vols. I-IV.
Tomaševskij, B. *Literatura i biografija* (Moscow, 1923).
Tschiževskij (Čiževskij), Dmitrij (ed.). *Russische literarische Parodien* (Wiesbaden: Otto Harrassowitz, 1957).
Tynjanov, Ju. *Arxaisty i novatory* (Leningrad: Priboj, 1929).
—, *Mnimaja poezija* (Moscow–Leningrad: Academia, 1931).
—, *Problema stixotvornogo jazyka* (Leningrad, 1924).
Wells, Carolyn (ed.). *A Parody Anthology* (New York: Scribners, 1932).
Žemčužnikov, A. M. *Izbrannye proizvedenija* (Moscow–Leningrad, 1963).
—, *Sočinenija v dvux tomax* (St. Petersburg, 1898).

ARTICLES AND PERIODICALS

Anon. "Polnoe sobranie sočinenij K. Prutkova S. Pb., 1884", *Delo*, No. 3 (1884), pp. 53-56.
Bergson, Henri. "Laughter", in *Comedy*. Edited by Wylie Sypher (New York: Doubleday and Co., 1956), pp. 61-190.
Berkov, P. N. "Neizdannye i zabytye proizvedenija Koz'my Prutkova", *Literaturnoe nasledstvo*, III (1932), 217-26.
Buxštab, B. Ja. "Estetizm v poezii 40-60 x rogob i parodii Koz'my Prutkova", Institut russkoj literatury. *Trudy otdela novoj russkoj literatury* (Moscow–Leningrad, 1948). I, 143-74.
—, "Koz'ma Prutkov, P. P. Eršov i N. A. Čižov", *Omskij almanax*, Bk. 5 (Omsk, 1945), pp. 116-130.
—, "Toržestvo dobrodeteli", *Literaturnoe nasledstvo*, LXVII (1959), 759-773.
Čiževskij, Dmitrij. "O literaturnoj parodii", *Novyj Žurnal*, No. 79 (June, 1965), pp. 118-140.
Čujko, V. V. "Jumoristy", in *Sovremennaja russkaja poezija v ee predstaviteljax* (Petersburg, 1885), pp. 175-78.

Fedorova, A. "Russkij Gejne", *Russkaja poezija XIX veka*. Edited by B. M. Ejxenbaum and Ju. N. Tynjanov (Leningrad: Academia, 1929), pp. 248-298.

Grossman, L. P. "Parodija kak žanr' literaturnoj kritiki", in *Russkaja literaturnaja parodija*. Edited by B. Begak, N. Kravcov, and A. Morozov (Moscow, 1930). pp. 39-48.

[Kugel', A. P.] Homo Novus, "Zametki", *Teatr i iskusstvo*, No. 3 (1913), pp. 65-68,

Kotljarevskij, N. A. "Starinnye portrety. Graf Aleksej Tolstoj kak satirik", *Vestnik Evropy*, IV (July, 1906), 5-48.

McLean, Hugh. "On the Style of a Leskovian Skaz", *Harvard Slavic Studies*, II (1954), 297-320.

Morozov, A. A. "Parodija kak literaturnyj žanr (k teorii parodii)", *Russkaja literatura*, No. 1 (1960), pp. 48-77.

[Pypin, A.] "Polnoe sobranie sočinenij Koz'my Prutkova S Pb. 1884", *Vestnik Evropy*, No. 3 (March, 1884), pp. 391-93.

Solov'ev, V. S. "Prutkov K. P.", in *Enciklopedičeskij slovar'*, XXV (Petersburg, 1898), 633-34.

Sovremennik. 1854, 1859-1863.

Vindt, Lidija. "Basnja kak literaturnyj žanr", *Poetika* (Leningrad, 1927). III, 87-101.

UNPUBLISHED MATERIALS

ANSSSR, Institut russkoj literatury. (Puškinskij dom, Leningrad). Rukopisnyj otdel. Notes by Vladimir Žemčužnikov in 1884 copy of Koz'ma Prutkov, *Polnoe sobranie sočinenij*.

Biblioteka imeni Lenina, Moscow. Rukopisnyj otdel, muzejnoe sobranie, Fond 101, 178.

Central'nyj gosudarstvennyj arxiv literatury i iskusstva (CGALI), Moscow. Fond 639.

INDEX